CLASSIFICATION: POETRY

A CIP catalogue record for this book is available from
the British Library.

Printed and bound in Great Britain.

Cover painting by William Hobson.

This West Midlands edition

ISBN 1-904169-64-3

First published in Great Britain in 2002 by
United Press Ltd
Admail 3735
London
EC1B 1JB
Tel: 0870 240 6190
Fax: 0870 240 6191
ISBN for complete set of volumes
1-904169-66-X
All Rights Reserved

www.upltd.co.uk

A
Passion
for
Poetry

Foreword

Look at life and you can't fail to be dazzled by its sheer complexity. Each person's life can be like a great poem - meaningful, memorable and unique.

But some people prefer to ignore life's complications and meander through their days in a daze. They would rather go through the motions of existence until they realise, too late, that they should have booked a seat on the rollercoaster of life rather than watch it flash by.

If you don't have a passion in your life, you have never lived. Different people choose different passions.

Some choose poetry, and the sheer diversity of the things they write about is clearly illustrated in this book. It brings together a group of poets who can express their passion for life in such a variety of ways.

I hope that in reading these verses you can find words which strike a chord in your heart, and unearth in you a new passion for poetry.

Peter Quinn, Editor.

Contents

The poets who have contributed to this volume are listed below, along with the relevant page upon which their work can be found.

	Daniel Ridgway	90	Pauline Brown
63	William Pyle		Debbie McLeod
64	Samantha Johnson	91	Lyn Smailes
	Heidi Charlotte	92	Emma Melville
	Brittlebank	93	Angela Dunsby
65	Cheryl Hulme	94	Becky Lucas
66	Cara Beckett	95	Yve Smithers
67	Wendy Simons		Margaret Power
	Lois Olivia Cooper		Burnip
68	Margaret Kaye	96	Pat Bidmead
69	Charlotte Merry		Anthony Emberger-
70	Kerry Beeston		Hughes
	Jane Armstrong	97	Christopher Smith
71	John Pegg		Sue J Bell
72	Jane Johns	98	Neil Phillips
	Nicola Regan	99	Victoria Brown
73	M Baxter		Simon Gunter
	Shirley Price	100	Alex Galloway
74	Kenneth Ginders		John Arnold
	Stephanie Abberley	101	Paul Kelly
75	Rose Starkie	102	Howard Lucas
76	Ian Challinor	103	Sheila Rogers
	Catherine Lambert	104	Carole Hare
77	Jackie O'Nions	105	Mayumi Rosalynd Tew
	Andrea Haynes	106	Faye Williams
78	Maureen Edden	107	Jean Russell
79	Ethel May Hatfield		John Jenkins
	Pamela Dyke	108	Laura Castree
80	Julie Copeland		Thomas Blundell
81	Joyce Thorley	109	Peter Hayling
	Jenkyn Evans	110	Hetvi Bhatt
82	Dorothy Chadwick		Kerry Smith
83	Frances Matten	111	Patricia Cousins
	Sylvia Dodds	112	L Kelley
84	Joan Wilde		Alan Davis
	Linda Timmis	113	Zoë Spencer
85	Joanne Rainbow		Kezia Thomas
86	Melanie Louise Heath	114	Elizabeth Rawson
	Victor Church	115	Sally Jobson
87	Faarea Masud	116	Linda Flowers
88	Angela Corrall		Alan Kavanagh
89	Kathryn Graham	117	Kevin Tonry
	Rita Carter		Jacqueline Burke

118	F Cutler
119	Jane Swain
	Godfrey Nall
120	Madeleine Williams
121	Paul Harris
122	Heather McCurry
	Katherine Parker
123	Anne Harding
	Samantha Ives
124	Dorothy Hunt
	Ann Wallace
125	Mark Dabbs
126	Aradhna Jaswal
127	Hena Begum
128	Louise Nutting
	Marian Latham
129	Steven Goodall
	Joan Morris
130	Alexandra Gail Millington
131	Steven G Powell
132	Wendy Glear
	Sabiha Ullah
133	M A Evans
134	Andrew Blakemore
135	Thomas White
136	Florence Thomas
	Claudine Weeks
137	Clive Bowen
138	Elizabeth White
	Gail Sturgess
139	Francis Harrison
140	Gillian Oakley
	Angela Kirby
141	Betty Wright
	Sarah Jones
142	Evette Johnston
	Jacqueline Sutton
143	Gemma Styles
	Luke Mosley
144	Julie Sheridan
	Thomas Ilsley
145	James Slater

146	Alexandra Weston
147	Alan J Woodhams
	Garry Thomas
148	John Carr
	Saajida Mehrali
149	James Turner
150	Louise Green
151	Ian Griffiths
152	Joan Garbett
	Gemma Martin
153	Peter Hill
154	Beryl Powles
	Melanie Dillon
155	Matthew Jackson
	Matthew Shilvock
156	Catherine Kerr
	M Nickson
157	Peter Hawkins
158	Stephen C Page
159	Geoffrey Hughes
	Mary McPhee
160	Anne-Marie McDonald
161	Mary Bagley
162	Betty Harper
	Anne Priest
163	Kirsty Saunders
	Clare Coleman
164	Mark Sanderson
	Stephen Holdnall
165	Dorothy Ann Parker
	Wendylyn Broadbent
166	Mahmuda Yasmin
167	Jean Spink
168	Robyn Mosley
	Malcolm Davies
169	Martin P Burns
170	Lorna Evans
171	Steve Urbanski
	Rosie Thomas
172	Nuressa Bessell
173	Joan Leggett
	Mike Cowsill
174	Virginia Hancock

175	Emma Louise Cartwright
	Sheila Manley
176	Oliver Thomas
	Joclyn Tolley
177	Derek Gardner
	Sreeman Barua
178	John C Bird
	R C Kelly
179	R Warrior
180	Beverley Hill
181	Rachel Evan
182	Helen Yendall
	Yvonne Bloor
183	Ivan Latham
	Winifred Saha
184	Alison Lowther
185	Louise Clay
186	Elisabeth Snelling
	R J Neale
187	Helen Brown
	Edward Kibbler
188	Rikki Nicholls
	David Clarke
189	Jacqueline Massey
	Beverley Welsh
190	Lisa Biddle
	Celia F Brown
191	Paul Portmann
	P J Kemp
192	Frank Pavitt
	Wendy Dedicott

FRIENDSHIP

Dearest friend where would I be
If by chance our paths had not crossed?
How emptiness would flourish free
My life you have richly embossed.

We have been through so many things
Over the years now surpassed,
The sadness, joy and many stings
Experiences made to last.

We've worked together, joked a while,
Spent many a day at leisure,
You've dealt with dignity and style
Those memories made to treasure.

Stories new, and stories to share
We've entertained our friends,
When we are in our rocking chairs
We'll have plenty of tales to lend.

Although with sadness we're apart,
My love to you I'll send,
Your picture's always in my heart
My dearest, dearest friend.

Julia L A Kelly, Hereford, Herefordshire

Julia Kelly said: "I have been writing in verse for the past five years and have been strongly influenced by the beautiful countryside of Herefordshire (the land of apples) where I was born and have always lived. In my opinion, having travelled far and wide, this part of the world is as close as you can get to Heaven without actually entering. In particular the tiny village of Bredwardine where I grew up and its wonderful down-to-earth residents, both past and present, have played a major part in giving me the inspiration to write my verses and to whom I will always be grateful. I am publishing a series of poetry books entitled 'Veracious Verses'. Book one is obtainable via email from: JKelly1147@aol.com."

WHY?

Coroner, coroner from what did she die?
Did something heavy fall from the sky?
Has she eaten a poisonous pie?
Did a witch put a splinter in her eye?
No, no young man, when push comes to shove The poor
unhappy maid died of unrequited love.

Jackie Davies, Redditch, Worcestershire

Born in Birmingham **Jackie Davies** enjoys driving, writing
poetry and songs. "I started writing verse as a young child
but did not keep any of my work," she remarked. "Only in
the last three years have I kept my poems and shown them
to others. My work is influenced by my own experience and
my style is romantic. I would like to be remembered as a
kind person." Aged 55, Jackie is a housewife with an ambi-
tion to write a piece of truly memorable poetry. She is mar-
ried to Les. "The person I would most like to meet is Jesus
because he is the greatest man ever to have lived," she
said. "As well as poems I have written two country songs.
My biggest fantasy is to live in the country in a sweet cot-
tage with roses around the door."

EMMANUEL

The silent anonymity of conception
Self-abnegates, as life utters
Into harmony with flesh and bone:
Grown onto rootstock of creation's own
Irrepressible fountain of possibility.

Diversity pulsates to the beat
Of the eternal drum,
cascading truth and certainty.

God's dream becomes the waking womb;
"I am" is echoed in all things;
And, in the silence,
Being sings its throbbing song
And trembles into life.

Paul Amphlett, Malvern, Worcestershire

GRANDSON WILLIAM

Oh, nannie what is this,
Oh, nannie, I need a kiss,
Then he sits upon my lap,
Then he has a little nap.

A lovely smile he gives to me,
"I love you nannie" to me, says he,
"I love you too, my little treasure,"
You always give me so much pleasure.

"Goodbye mum, see you later today,
My nan, and me, need to play,"
A wonderful game of make believe life,
Far away from this life of strife.

What shall we do, what shall we make,
On with the oven, let's make a cake,
What a time we have had with this,
The cake a success, then another kiss.

What shall we do now nannie, sing a song or two,
Play a game just us two,
Let's build a den just for us,
Then we can play from morn, till dusk.

Patricia Appleton, Redditch, Worcestershire

WALKING

When I'm walking in the woodland, my dogs running on
ahead
The wind blowing gently through my hair
I feel as though I haven't a care
Happy thoughts whirl through my head.

There's something about the countryside that makes me
glad I'm alive
Is it the trees, the grass, the flowers or the birds' songs, the
squirrel or the sky?
Could it be that I feel content and privileged to be able to
see this beauty?
Whatever it is, it sets my spirits high.

My cheeks glow, my heart feels light
I feel refreshed, invigorated, happy
Even if I once was sad
When I've finished my walk, my heart is glad
It's very therapeutic you see
My dogs, the woods, the wildlife and me.

Wendy Rachel Bransby, Bromsgrove, Worcestershire

*Dedicated to Len Bransby. I'm so happy you are part of my
life. I will love you always.*

BIRDS AND CHEESE

I aim to please and here is
Another wheeze, about the
Birds and the bees

Also it's about a man with
Exploding knees because he
Eats too many bees

They had to be extracted
With some cheese what a
wheeze

Don't be sad be glad you
Know a crazy fool like me.

Richard Griffith, Redditch, Worcestershire

CURTAIN CALL

The audience clapped on, loudly
Came whistles and shouts of more.
Six curtain calls took I, in all
Then a wave from the wings,
Encore

The curtain rose, again I bowed.
Stood humble, in emotion wrought;
What an exhilarating sound,
Enlivened by a loud report

The people screamed, with great delight
Seeing a pistol poised at me,
A little lad, defiantly
Shouting, "Say when, mum, count-two, three."

Patricia Hale, St Johns, Worcestershire

WORCESTER CITY

Of Worcester's Guild-hall stand and see,
Three English monarchs Queen Anne, Charles one,
Charles two, but not Charles three.
Of the high street with Elgar's statue standing firm,
Viewing the cathedral's mighty stone hulk.
Of King John's tomb, may he rest in heaven.
See the Severn, England's longest river, from City Bridge,
Or The New Road's cricket ground beneath the cathedral's
benevolent gaze.
Of Worcester's Pitchcroft racecourse, horses to see.
And uncountable wonders as well to see.
Worcester, oh Worcester, is good enough for me.

K I Squires, Worcester, Worcestershire

TO LOVE ONLY ONCE

So many years ago,
It seems like yesterday.
His face, his smile, his eyes, the smell of him
Memories that have never left me.

I lived for him, to see him.
The day I left
"All the best", the closing of a door
Slowly, as if
Time
Had
Stopped.
I watched that door
But he never came back

I never forgot him, I never will
But I hope that I won't
Love only once.

Kirsty Anne Wilkes, Kidderminster, Worcestershire

EARTHS WONDERS

You gave me the moonbeams you gave me the rains.
You gave me the sunlight and the leafy lanes.
Everything to confront us as we wake in the morn.
Tantalising colours from the sunrays adorn.

You gave us the stars you gave us the nights.
You gave us the snowflakes that brighten the dark nights.
You gave us the trees meadows for the cows.
Everything on earth our wealth the Lord He endowed.

You gave us the winter, autumn, summer and spring
You gave us the strength and wonderful voices to sing.
We sing about love, romance we adore
You gave us the knowhow to travel the world's floors.

Rivers and trees, typhoons and breezes
Birds, dogs, horses and fish.
God you gave us everything that we mortals would wish.
We blame the devil for everything bad.
But we mortals are the ones who make everything bad.

Derrick Bright, Worcester, Worcestershire

Derrick Bright said: "I was born in 1931 and educated at a Catholic school. My interests include songwriting, football, and cricket and I have been writing poetry for ten years. I also write beautiful songs using poetry as the lyrics then progress my words and music into lovely songs. I am married to Jean and we have three sons. I would love to meet Sarah Brightman and sing a duet with her. I have written hundreds of poems and have had many published."

WHO AM I TO?

Who am I to judge others?
When I cannot judge myself,
Who am I to fear the dark?
When it cannot be seen,
Who am I to fear the light?
When it shows the way ahead,
Who am I to be afraid of criticism?
When fear is the enemy of creativity.
Who am I to be afraid of ridicule?
When laughter could be envy dressed up,
Who am I?
I am who I am, me a gift to myself.

Kenneth Powell, Worcester, Worcestershire

THE POWER OF TOUCH

He took her hand in his, so gentle, yet so strong,
Their hands together beside her head,
He sat next to her upon her bed.
The closeness felt, the warmth in her heart,
Their souls had joined and would never be apart.
As he left he looked her in the eye, then kissed her lips
gently
And said goodbye,
That first simple, yet special kiss
Now forever locked in her heart, would always be in her
memories,
Even though they are now apart.

Lynsey Tocker, Redditch, Worcestershire

*The flowers lasted a while, but the memory of your support
and kindness that day, will last forever.*

A POEM'S LIKE LIFE

A poem written to please
can tantalise and tease
any subject can be read with ease
even if written with great speed

A poem written with sorrow can bring a tear
or when written with love is for all to hear
a poem can be all your fear
or even bring someone near

Poems are just like life
full of feelings, full of strife
so fill your head with rhyme
and poems that are sublime.

Suzann Milnes, Ross-on-Wye, Herefordshire

Born in Ross-on-Wye **Suzann Milnes** is a mother of two
with an ambition to have as many experiences as possible.
"I started writing poetry for a competition because my
daughter encouraged me to enter," she explained. "My work
is influenced by everyday experiences and my style is real-
istic. I would like to be remembered for having the courage
to do new things, like writing poetry." Aged 29, Suzann
would most like to meet the comedian Graham Norton. "I
would like to see if he is as much fun in real life as he is on
the screen," she said. "I would love to be a historian but my
biggest fantasy is to win the lottery."

FROM NIGHT TO DAY

Perpetual stars emit their glow
Showering light to the earth below
Giving direction strength and peace
Symbols of love that will never cease
The hush of night gives way to first light
Heavenly charm is dismissed from sight
Fluffy clouds disappear from view
As glorious sunshine pushes through

Philip O'Leary, Redditch, Worcestershire

THE TRAFFIC WARDEN

He pounds the streets all the long day
Oh, how I wish he'd go away
With his coat of yellow and cap on his head
He's going to book you, no matter what's said.

His eyes light up, gleaming with pleasure
I've got him weighed up, I've got his measure
Strolling around with his notebook and pen
He got you once, he'll get you again.

He comes down the road, face lit up with a smile
He doesn't care, you've only been there a while
When he gives you a ticket which means you'll be fined
You need to show him that you don't really mind.

Don't show that warden that you even care
Accept his ticket with deadly stare
Now smile back at him to upset his day
And give him a wave as you drive away.

Jean Taylor, Worcester, Worcestershire

SILENCE OF TRANQUILLITY

The day job done, the journey homeward bound
By car, bus, train, the walk to match the key
With home, sweet home, that ever-welcome sight.
And thus achieved, then fresh-brewed cup of tea.

Sitting, sipping, thinking on the day,
An overwhelming stillness fills the void
With fond embrace and soft intensity.
So are the day's frustrations full destroyed.

The healing strength of silence strikes the soul
With deafening impact targeting the core.
No doctor's needed daily to prescribe
This natural medicine eager to restore.

Christopher Carter, Stourport-on-Severn, Worcestershire

Christopher Carter said: "I have written occasional verses
for many years for my own amusement. My poems need a
rhythm to enhance the message that they carry, be they
jokey greetings-card rhymes, or more serious statements.
As a retired veterinary surgeon, I have been privileged to
meet many people and touch on their own emotional expe-
riences. I am sure this has influenced my understanding of
our fragile existence. I have had three poems published in
anthologies of veterinary verse and have also written music
for organ and for piano, some with accompanying verses."

COUNTING THE SNAILS

Counting the snails that pass through my life
Watching the slugs cross the road
Measuring my life at caterpillar's pace
Saving the worms from pavement cracks
Small movements and creatures of my life.
Moving images creeping thru' my mind
Extraordinary memories fill my dreams
Films I should not have seen
Books I should not have read
How to live with the bad parts of reality?
How to sleep with such pictures on my pillow?

Margot Miller, Fownhope, Herefordshire

Margot Miller said: "I have written most of my poetry in the last ten years since moving from the Cotswolds to Glastonbury, Somerset and then to Fownhope, Herefordshire. I am inspired by the spirit of the landscape. I use the seasonal changes in the countryside as a backdrop to my writing. I am very interested in the Celtic Iron Age period, and have recently published a historical novel set in this period called 'The Priestess of Ennor' which includes my poetry. My next book to be published in the US concerns the Celtic ogham tree alphabet."

IT STARTED WITH A KISS

Where are my frogs and
Who are my princes?
Why are they now just a
Memory
Of jelly and quinces in a
Garden of small
Delight?
The frogs swim together
Still
In a life's procreative plan.
The princes all are vanished
And only left is a man
Of few words
In the soft starry night.

C V Nethersole, Hereford, Herefordshire

ELIZABETH

In 1953, I was six,
Peering at the flickering telly
Watching a fairytale coach.
Everything in black and white.
Trying to keep still on a stool.

We learnt about Australia
Where the Queen toured.
Mum showed us photos
Of blonde curly-haired Anne.

Now it's 2002,
Our daughter is in Melbourne,
Our children are grown.
It only seems yesterday
And the Queen looks the same.

Jane Cox, Leominster, Herefordshire

HELP ME

What's that noise I can hear on the green?
They tell me it's the children at play.
There's the smack of the ball against the net.
Everyone shrieks, a goal, I bet!
The excitement's intense. "We've won," they say.
I wish I could see.

I sit on the bench. At the other end
A mother tends her fractious child, they say
The crying of the child makes me sad.
It stops. "They've moved away," they say.
I wish I could see.

Now the barking of a dog,
"A poodle pup and a ball," they say.
His owner shrieks with joy
"He's got it now, you naughty boy."
I wish I could see.

Oh, a beautiful sound makes me glad,
What is it? "A cuckoo," they say.
It's repetitive sounds fills me with glee.
I want to run and run and feel perfectly free!
Oh I wish I could see.

Petal Mary O'Hea, Hereford, Herefordshire

Petal Mary O'Hea said: "I have spent my adult life teaching poetry and helping people to love it. I've travelled the world examining for Trinity College of Music, holding workshops on speech, drama and effective speaking, different poetry periods and interpretation. I've contributed to the Living Faith Section in local newspapers and radio and have published articles in book form. Two books of poetry have been published. Anthologies and 'The Lady' have published my work. People and nature matter passionately to me and, like Wordsworth, I believe a poet hath put his heart to school."

WHAT'S IN A NAME?

Winifred, Winifred, how she hates that name
Mummy gave it to her before the fashion changed.

Winifred, Winifred, in the 'twenties it was chic,
But now we're in the 'nineties and it makes her want to
shriek.

Winifred, Winifred, how it grates upon her ears,
If only they had stopped to think, she'd carry it for years.

Winifred, Winifred, a name that's hardly racey,
But worse, mum could have changed her mind and made it
Shaz, or Tracey.

Take comfort, dearest Winifred, and don't you change an
ounce,
It's not the name that makes the girl, it's what's inside that
counts.

Gordon Mayling, Bromsgrove, Worcestershire

Born in Woburn Sands **Gordon Mayling** enjoys philately and
watercolour painting. "I started writing poetry in 1992 follow-
ing near-death illnesses and time spent convalescing," he
explained. "My work is influenced by human nature and my
style is both whimsical and humorous. I would like to be
remembered kindly and with love." Aged 69, he is retired but
has an ambition to die at the age of 110 at the hands of a jeal-
ous lover! He is married to Mary and they have two daughters.
"I would love to be the Chancellor of the Exchequer for a day
and the person I would most like to meet is Mick Jagger to
discover how debauched I need to become to earn a knight-
hood," he said.

THE MINER

Dawn has still to break as he walks the six miles to the colliery.
On aged legs he has wrapped thick brown paper tied with string to keep them dry.
On his shoulder his tommy bag carries his can of water and meagre lunch.

The cage creaks and judders as it descends the shaft.
Rats scuttle past while he kneels in water digging into the coalface, or lying on his belly clawing out the lumps.
With only the light from the carbide lamp on his hat, he shovels the coal into the trolley, swallowing the dust that hangs in the air.

The hooter sounds the end of another day
And wearily he climbs into the cage, his face black, his mouth dry,
Walking the well-worn path home
His thoughts drift to his family waiting for him
And the tin bath filled with hot water in front of the fire
Ready to wash away the day's grime.

Margaret Darrington, Ross-on-Wye, Herefordshire

THE ANCIENT WRECK

I walked a lonely path
A wide open vista,
Of windmills and yachts,
And low wooden fences,
Here, on English land.

The sun was warm,
It invited me to sit.
Taught me to wait.

I found a wreck
Of a very old ship,
It creaked and groaned.
The water bumped it.

Angela Jane Porter, Kidderminster, Worcestershire

STATION

It's a place for softly sighing and poignant final goodbyes,
a platformed land of receding images and
gentle moistened eyes.

Perhaps it's somewhere for contemplating
exactly who's to blame,
while enduring lengthening shadows,
waiting for a train.

Solitarily staring at this drab accoutrement of steel rail cre-
ation,
persuaded nothing in existence forlornly
haunts like an empty railway station.

Nick Dyer, Evesham, Worcestershire

*Dedicated to my darling wife Michelle, always an inspira-
tion, especially on those less than sunny days.*

PATTERNS

Splash, a raindrop falls into the lake.
A single drop and a pattern begins.
A rippling circle, a wave of force.
Pushing ever outwards
In an endless, timeless rhythm.

Splash, another and another.
And soon the circles merge and swirl.
Mingling together until the lake becomes
Alive and vital, pulsating with a force
That only raindrops bring.

Splash, a drop of kindness falls into the lake.
The lake of life, where much is greed and hate.
More drops and the patterns begin
Concentric waves of life pulsating
In an endless, timeless rhythm.

Splash, compassion, wisdom, love
Mingling together until the lake becomes
Alive and vital, pulsating with hope
Fostering love, that banishes greed and hate,
Which only kindness brings.

Audrey Brown, Worcester, Worcestershire

Born in Lancashire **Audrey Brown** enjoys music, needlecraft and writing. Now 74 and a widow she is a retired teacher. "Since my husband died I just wanted to take life easy, travel, pursue my musical abilities, spend time with my children and grandchildren and continue writing," she explained. "My husband was a victim of Alzheimer's disease and I have written articles for the Alzheimer's Society and my own book 'A Matter of Timing' ISBN 185776 331 9 which is the story of my husband's illness and how my family coped with it."

PILLOW

It's 5 am in the morning.
I hear the front door close.
So I cuddle the pillow that lies here beside me,
In the place where your body once lay.
I cuddle the pillow that holds your smell near to me,
Hoping that it will stay.
I cuddle the pillow that held your dear head,
And I reach for that pillow warm in my bed.
And I remember our bodies softly entwined,
As I watched you sleep on that pillow of mine.
And cuddling that pillow loving memories I keep.
Fresh from this morning, right through to next week.

Carol Graham, Hereford, Herefordshire

OPPOSITE

For every thing there is an opposite,
For life there is death,
For black there is white,
For you there is me,
Opposites surround our world,
Yet we are oblivious to them.
For a planet in space there is no planet,
For the black hole there is a white hole,
For love there is hate,
There is an opposite to every living thing.
Opposites make us who we are.
So be proud of who you are I am.

Carrie-Anne Hollywell, Kings Pyon, Herefordshire

Carrie-Anne Hollywell said: "I now reside in Herefordshire after moving from Gloucestershire four years ago. I love to write stories and poetry. I'm 13 years old and my ambition is to become a fully-fledged writer."

BEFORE YOU

I feel no dread of the sunset
Nor yet of the waning moon,
I have no fear of the cold sheets
Laid across my body too soon.

And as for the tears of my dearest
They bring me no sorrow at all.
They fill me with joy at the love felt,
As they sparkle and glisten and fall,

I'll leave you too soon I do fancy
I'll leave you depleted by some,
And I'll sit in the sunlight before you
And I'll sit, and I'll wait till you come.

Colin Christian, Bromyard, Herefordshire

THE TRINITY OF WHATEVER

Was this man of lowly birth
God's beloved son
Virgin womb entrusted
Or carpenter blessed
Was He the man
Knowingly acting God's will
To be Judas-kissed
Thorn-crowned
Crucified to everlasting glory
Or was He the man
Uncertain, ordinary with fear
For Himself and mankind
Yet Trinity or whatever,
There is the certainty of His eternal love.

Idwal Davies, Kidderminster, Worcestershire

HALLO?

The thought occurs while on the phone
That you are never quite alone,
That anyone from far or near,
A cousin, aunt, one you hold dear
Or just a man from double glazing
Who times it right, it is amazing,
Just as you start to eat your food
Will call you up, you then are rude
And you end up with indigestion
How to have peace, that is the question.

A perfect stranger rings your number
And wakes you up from deepest slumber
Who hails you loudly with great glee
And calls you George and shouts it's me
At last he's gone, all's quiet and still,
You wish you had a sleeping pill,
You lie awake and ponder deep
And tell yourself, before you sleep
The set that keeps us all in touch
At times does so by far too much.

Ursula Mills, Hereford, Herefordshire

THE RAIN IS FALLING

The rain is falling it's now getting dark
Perhaps in a few months we will be able
To walk in the park,
Until then it may freeze again
We will look forward to a gentle breeze
Flood's all round upon the ground
Sunshine may peak we have
A gentle sneak.
Few months away it's sunshine all the day
Please not too hot.
The flies will get into a knot
So now we sleep into the dark
Then tomorrow I'll take the dog.
To the park.

Pauline Millman, Kidderminster, Worcestershire

LAMENT FOR A LOST LOVE

Night time has fallen and across the dark hill
The rustling of grass and whippoorwill shrill
The chirp of a cricket and the old barn owl's "whoo"
All stirring memories my sweet love of you.

As I lie on my back looking at the dark sky
Where are you my love my soul seems to cry.
I miss your sweet kiss when you held my face
The nearness of you in our secret place

You are gone from my sight but not from my heart
No distance or space or time can us part.
You may have passed on to a new world somewhere
But tarry my darling I'll meet with you there.

Joan Gallen, Redditch, Worcestershire

A LOVING RELATIONSHIP

Enriched by the beauty of God's great creation
I prayed for a relationship based on a firm foundation
God answered my need, he sent you to me
Rescued from loneliness, I was made free

I was yours forever, and forever you were mine
Our pulsated happiness sped through space and time
Then came the parting, separated we were
Near each other no longer, me in silence and tear

My emotional state had an ebb and a flow
Your love was worth more than words can ever know
Faced with a truth that I must go on without you
Somehow I'll manage, truly, I will get through

In the garden at eventide, I sit down to dream
Of you beside me, recalling a love so supreme
Such devotional care within the breast was found
That the worship for each other was deeply sound

William Turberfield, Ledbury, Herefordshire

Born in Birmingham, **William Turberfield** enjoys poetry, gardening and walking. "I stated writing poetry as a child and I would describe my style as creative," he explained. "I would like to be remembered as a caring person and my ambition is to be a better man each day." Aged 70, he is a retired NHS worker. He is married to Enid and they have five children. "The person I would most like to be for a day is the poet laureate and I would most like to meet Queen Elizabeth," he said. "I have written short stories and a large number of poems, many of which have been published."

A SIMPLE THANKSGIVING

For turnips and peas and tall leafy trees
I give you grateful thanks O Lord
for fingers and toes sweet smells for my nose
for chuckling babies and large smiling ladies
for a soft summer breeze cats and dogs without fleas
I give you grateful thanks O Lord

for socks without holes and achieving my goals
I give you grateful thanks O Lord
for a house and bed and curls on my head
for oceans and rocks and bright summer frocks
for burgers and fries the sound of gulls in the skies
I give you grateful thanks O Lord

for friend and foe and especially Jo
I give you grateful thanks O Lord
for music and verse and plays to rehearse
for books and TV and folks who love me
for limericks and prose and an afternoon doze
I give you grateful thanks O Lord

Jean Morgan Fisk, Redditch, Worcestershire

AT SEVENTY

Having reached my allotted span
of three score years and ten.
I'm beginning to wonder if I can
take up the challenge and wield my pen

I would really like to be a poet
To quote good verse at any time
I hope my writing doesn't show it
but I feel as if I'm committing a crime

How dare I think that I can write
I'm much too old and potty
In fact my family are probably right
They think I'm slightly dotty.

They are very good at suffering me
and encouraging me to create,
to stop me feeling all at sea
and thinking I've left it far too late

Hooray for being seventy
and doing what you wish
nonsense fills my head a-plenty
for poetry's a heady dish.

Pamela Bryan, Ross-on-Wye, Herefordshire

Pamela Bryan said: "I have been writing poetry for eight
years, since I became a widow. I have a large, truly loving fam-
ily who have encouraged me to write. I hope one day to be able
to publish my own collection of poems as I have had poems in
many anthologies. I love the countryside, gardens, family and
friends and all of my poems reflect these themes, although
certain occasions of note also inspire me, such as the death of
Princess Diana, the Queen mum's 100 birthday, the Queen's
Jubilee and writing poems for peace. I also enjoy reading and
dabbling in painting."

BENEATH THIS SKIN

My love, my darling, how I long to feel
You touch my hair, my cheek, caress my chin;
Beneath this wrinkled skin there still is me,
My soul, my life are just the same within.
Can you not see the need I have for you
To love me and not see that I am old?
Reach out to me; I'm not so far away.
I feel so lonely out here in the cold.
Is love just for the young and fair of face?
I love you. Hold me close and show you care.
My heart still beats; it longs for your embrace;
The girl you loved and cherished is still there
Beneath this skin.

Rosemary Jordan, Stourport-on-Severn, Worcestershire

PEACE WITHIN

She was old, very old.
She was blind, very blind
But her heart it was great and gay.
For her life had been filled with the joy of youth
In her day.

She had loved very well,
She had lived very long,
And her sons they were wise and strong;
They clustered around her like moths round a light,
Such a throng.

Her teeth they were few, very few.
Her hands they were frail and thin
But her smile was of sweet content
And the light in her eyes told of love and of
Peace within.

Flora Hughes, Ross-on-Wye, Herefordshire

RAINWALKERS

Are you old enough
to know what a collar stud
looks like?
My father wore one
to fasten his stiff white collar
to his shirt,
And I as a child
sat on the window seat
and watched the raindrops
as they plopped on to the pavement
sending up button heads.
Just like collar studs
or maybe rainwalkers

Winifred Mills, Ross-on-Wye, Herefordshire

THE INTRUDER

I didn't mean to do it,
But he gave me a surprise
When he crept into my bedroom
And stood right before my eyes.

I was all alone that night,
No one there who I could call
To give me some assistance
As he ran close by the wall.

So I picked up my slipper,
And as he advanced towards my bed,
I gave him one quick blow
And the spider fell down dead.

Christine Shakespeare, Stourport-on-Severn, Worcestershire

TEA-ROOM

Pain across the tea cups.
Tense silences wiped away with indifferent chatter
Eyes don't meet much now,
And when, avert quickly to another matter.
Once in this spoon-tinkling, plate-scraping world,
A moment like this stood eternally still.
Tiny occurrences were neither seen nor heard.
A single gaze was needed, not more.
Now so many other faces to explore.
Cream cakes in sweet excess,
Briefly catch attention
Not enough really, to fill the fallen silence.
But tea is poured and the bill will soon be paid.
We'll be gone wishing we could have stayed.

David Burridge, Ross-on-Wye, Herefordshire

Dedicated to Helga. You bought the tea and encouraged me.

Born in London **David Burridge** enjoys writing poetry,
keeping fit and listening to jazz. "I have been writing on
and off for years but it is only recently that I have begun to
take my poetry and myself seriously," he explained. "I
would describe my style as both cynical and romantic and I
would like to be remembered as a very human person who
wanted his poetry to express that fact." Aged 56, he is a
personnel director with an ambition to discover himself in
his work, relationships and poetry. "The persons I would
most like to meet are the poets, Wendy Cope and V A
Fanthorpe because their work is gently human," he added.

WINTER HOPE

I've filled the peanut holders, piled high the bird table
and smashed the bird-bath ice.
Now bossy robins, pugnacious tits
and operatic blackbirds resting till next season
are momentarily content,
whilst I, my daily routine done,
sometimes resent my chosen servitude.
But, come the spring I know I will be paid
a thousand times with golden notes,
and dawning trust of nestlings newly fledged

Dorothy Williams, Malvern, Worcestershire

THE MASKING

Regarding this life from hollow eyes
The masks I wear have been my spies,
They've seen me laugh, they've seen me cry,
They've seen reality make a lie.
Before I leave,
I'd like to breathe
Everything I could not perceive.
From beginning to end
I wish I could mend
The broken parts,
Paint flaking hearts.
Masks have to die,
Have to say goodbye,
Have to crumble and crack
The old one's back.
This one is held fast
It will always last,
For it is mine,
All of the time.

Dawn Garey, Redditch, Worcestershire

MOTHER NATURE'S PLAYTIME

Dawn breaks and the garden comes alive
with the sound of Mother Nature awakening
fledglings with fluffy coats sit with beaks open
Waiting helplessly for breakfast to arrive
Their parents swooping to catch unsuspecting grubs
or picking berries that resemble polished gems
Squirrels scurrying from branch to branch, tails twitching
Shiny black eyes questioning any movement in their play-
ground
Leaves crinkle as a hedgehog trudges through undergrowth
curling into a prickly ball when danger is sensed
flowers start opening petals, with the warm morning sun
showing vibrant tones, rich reds and flame burnt orange
Spiders spinning silky threads and sun's early rays
Catch the webs like fine silver chains
When wintry weather falls, the first covering of snow,
fresh, until the tracks of animals disturb the pureness
As day grows lighter, people take over, no appreciative
glance,
Their minds lost in different worlds
The beauty will go unnoticed until dawn comes again
And animals will play in their secret garden.

Anita Longmuir, Bromsgrove, Worcestershire

Anita Longmuir said: "I love writing poetry and ghost sto-
ries and it is a great experience to have one of my poems
printed. My ultimate ambition is to have a book published.
My passion is reading. Recently I began a proof-reading
and copy-editing course which gives me the perfect oppor-
tunity to have my nose constantly stuck in a book. My
favourite genre is horror, but any page-turner which keeps
me quiet will find a permanent place on my bookshelf. My
fiancé, Paul, gives me the encouragement to feel confident
about my writing."

ROSE GARDEN

Warm from the sun
the stone bench
rested our noses.
We'd plunged into the silk,
folded sheets of petals,
like bees.
Intoxicated with citrus and myrrh.
Each one inhaled.
Each one shared,
like our dreams.

Clare Harrison, Evesham, Worcestershire

FLIGHT OF TYRANNY

Squabbling, chasing, threatening, with many a vicious
peck,
The blackbird who claims our garden
Will allow no rivals of his kind.
They fly in quite boldly, to the breadcrumbs on the lawn
Poor daddy blackbird leads a hope forlorn, as
They cram their beaks with pieces, while he advances from
behind
And they flutter in large circles, grabbing all they find.
Poor Mr Blackbird is so keen to chase them off
He never gets a bite himself, tho' there really is enough.
Sometimes he is so human in his funny, violent way,
As he lives in fields of plenty but keeps others all away.

Ian Kerley, Ross-on-Wye, Herefordshire

NO TEARS, JUST SMILE

No tears will you cry, put a smile on your face.
Now that I rest in a peaceful place,
Remember sometimes, if you've got a while,
The good times we all had,
Now give me a smile.

Hilary B Price, Orcop, Herefordshire

ACTUALLY DARLING

Actually darling I think you're quite sweet
But why must you hassle me each time we meet?
Actually darling I'm sure that one day
You'd like to grab me and take me away
To some other life which is all your idea
But actually darling I'm quite happy here
Actually darling I think of you often
But that doesn't mean that I haven't forgotten
The times when you ran around all over town
Leaving me lonely and weary and down
Actually darling I'm a good friend to you
But I do not think you've been honest and true
Actually darling you say that you'll stay
But I know that quite soon you'll be running away
Actually darling you can be so cold
And I'm thinking our friendship may suddenly fold
Actually darling I think I'll just leave
If I do darling I know you won't grieve
A friendship is good that survives all of this
So as I am leaving I'll blow you a kiss

Florence Maher, Leominster, Herefordshire

HEREFORD'S CROWNING GLORY

The cathedral stands so proud this day.
Whilst not letting time stand in it's way.
People take pictures of an architect's dream.
A stunning example, shrouded with green.

Different shades peep out, from amongst it's stone
A building this strong stands out on it's own.
The people of Hereford, how lucky you are
With a crown of your own, that's the best by far.

Who'd of thought, more jewels could be found
But Hereford's history and wealth does abound.
So not only a crown, but also its jewels.
Like the river called Wye, and the murky castle pool.

To look and treat well, not fill full of litter.
Would leave a sweet taste, not making it bitter.
The cathedral's for everyone to treasure and admire
History surrounds us with love and desire.

Hereford's people, the proud, keeper's you are
Leave others so envious as they travel from afar.
The crown and its jewels, if we keep at their best
Will ultimately keep us ahead of the rest.

Pat Potter, Hereford, Herefordshire

FREEDOM REGAINED

As the rain runs
Catching the whisper of your thought
As you turn in the dark of night
Love is forlorn
As the water falls from the hills
So I will regain my freedom
As the moon glimpses through shadows
The briefest of light
So my mind catches the same
As the river flows
Coldest of water runs naked across me
As the wind bends the lightest of branches
Of the strongest of trees
I finally face the day free

Stephen Mark French, Woodrow South, Worcestershire

Born in Albrighton, **Stephen French** enjoys writing, gardening and family life. "I started writing poetry about 20 years ago to express my feelings. My work is influenced by my life experiences and my style is passionate. I would like to be remembered as an emotional, thoughtful and compassionate person," he said. Aged 45, Stephen has an ambition to live a full and healthy life. He and his partner, Sue, who have two children, are due to be married in 2003. "The person I would most like to meet is Sir John Betjeman and I would love to be an American Indian for a day," said Stephen. "As well as many poems, I have also written song lyrics."

STILL BLOOMING WAITING

Sleeping petals fly away
no chance to say goodbye
leaving only memories
embers of love that refuse to die.

Burst kisses crush ribs so tight
temporary tears that try to soothe
but flood the nerves, no feelings
claiming no longer to lose.

Wake the hidden phoenix
a re-birth in my life
to chase away the cuckoo
who clasps the winged roses' knife.

Donna-Marie Robertson, Whittington, Shropshire

LIFE

We have the chance to show who
We are, make a name for us all,
And become a star,
But no matter what your life's to be,
Life is such a mystery,
Life is the hardest job of all,
We all work as individuals each and all,
What to do, what to see
But in the end it's all down to me.

Sandra Davies, Whitchurch, Shropshire

TROUBLE AND MY FRIEND

Every day I play with him,
he helps me into trouble
We went to the park,
and landed in a puddle.
I can't find a name for him.
but we have such a lark.

If only we could play each day,
just as mummy told me to.
We played in the farmer's hay
where I lost me new shoe.

Oh if only he would not let me,
get in so much trouble.
But then again it's mostly me.
For you see the trouble
It's not his fault at all,
he is only me shadow.

Hilary Cadogan, Oswestry, Shropshire

REVELATIONS

There is a lantern in a window;
A yellow glow from a crack in the blackness;
A moving, wheedling warmth, too far away to feel,
Provoking me to draw nearer,
And as I do, the crack grows bigger and the glow more
shiny,
And rays shimmer from the unknown light and search me
out,
And those who seek the night will see me bright like the
lantern,
And will know the heat of a candle flame,
And I will light up the night as I draw close to the window,
And our brightnesses will meet there in safe, revealing soli-
tude.

Frances G Day, Craven Arms, Shropshire

THIS WELSH CORNER

Once as a boy my father took my hand
and led me long the coast and the shoulder
Where through his lips the sea would speak
of its legend like a fire through water,
Oh whispered betrayal at the edge of the world
as a child here I folded in wonder.
And we gave a great roar to the chanting and blind
who first here dreamt of this corner.
For when I was young to the dark of the sun
I would leap to amaze in the words.
Where the laid out men held fast their enigma
like dust on the once-ancient fields,
I shall keep this secret in the knocking chest
buried cross a time and a yearning.
Baptised born of the double-crossed heart
I conceived of the hand and the burning.

Ryan Jones, Oswestry, Shropshire

THE MOTHER

Contentedly she watched him play
his childhood games throughout the day.
Delighting in her joy to see
his fun and boundless energy.
But when the toy gun that he found
had sent him flattened to the ground
in likeness of a soldier's pose,
her eyes and her expression froze.
It was as if, in him, she'd seen
the fodder for some war machine.

Margaret Whitaker, Shrewsbury, Shropshire

SHATTERED DREAMS

I gave my heart and you gave yours,
So long ago it seems,
And to my young mind you were then
The answer to my dreams.
We jogged along and seemed to be
The perfect match to all,
But it was very different
In practise I recall.
You ruled the roost
Took all my trust.
Betrayed me in the end.
And every opportunity
You took to re-offend.
You had your fun,
The magic's gone
There's nothing left for me.
Love's had its day
I'll go my way.
It's over now, I see.

Lilian Parker, Telford, Shropshire

UNCONVENTIONAL BEHAVIOUR

Off one's rocker
Out of one's mind
Taken leave of my senses
Left my reason behind

Time seems out of sync
All I seem to do is think
Brain balance on the brink
All because it's on the blink

Katy Rogers, Shrewsbury, Shropshire

TELFORD TILL I DIE

Suddenly it was in the papers one day,
front page feature in the Independent, lead story on
Newsnight.
But reporters and camera crews took off like birds in flight
and the town could be ignored, once more.

Who's left to witness the sight
of flowers placed each week and wrapped so tight;
hugging the grieving railings,
honouring a young man who died through others' failings.
As if love alone might bring him back to life.

Here in the Midlands' melting-pot
of black, white, Irish, Welsh and Scots,
I saw they used the yellow bars,
the cowards chose their time, their hour
to strike and then deny their crime.
While those who blunder don't resign
and we leave petitions blank, unsigned.

Neil Halliday, Telford, Shropshire

TEDDY BEARS

I have a small teddy bear,
Who has an awful lot of hair.
When he plays with his friend,
He drives me round the bend.

He sleeps at seven,
And dreams he is in heaven.
Sometimes he awakes in the night
When he has had an awful fright.

He wakes in the morning,
Just as the day is dawning.

Amy-Jayne Gardner, Broseley, Shropshire

INDULGENCE

Indulgence is a chocolate drink at four,
instead of tea and what is more,
the dunking of chocolate coated bickies,
to melt the coating and be licked is,
a flouting of the law
of etiquette and dietary lore.
A drag at a fag with drawling jaw,
ash into dregs of tea cup flicked is,
Indulgence.

To talk and talk and be the bore
at captive audience parties where,
all yawns ignored and ankles kicked is.
Ideas, beliefs and hopes nit picked is,
unanswered telephone messages more
Indulgence.

Janet Pinto, Telford, Shropshire

FREEDOM

A sprinkling of rain, brings new life again.
On a dry and barren land.
A dove takes flight, into the light.
Across the golden sand.
A time, a place, a smile on your face.
A twinkling in your eye.
Free to choose, you know you can't lose.
So why not give it a try,
A walk, a stroll, a new-born foal.
Freedom, at its call.
Life, so long, a voice, a song.
A reason not to fall.
Hand in hand, across the land.
Two lovers are, as one.
A harmony, a secret key.
Unlocks the midday sun.
Your gaze, a stare, your hidden flair.
Beauty held within.
So flowing free, a memory.
A moment, you can win.

Gini Knight, Market Drayton, Shropshire

Born in Chippenham **Gini Knight** enjoys photography, music, trekking on the West Coast of America and writing poetry. "I started composing poems in 1988 when I lived by the sea in Cornwall," she explained. "I just began to write down my thoughts and feelings and life and the state of the world. I am inspired by the songs of U2 and would describe my style as meaningful. I hope people can relate to my poems." Gini works in the retail industry and her ambition is for the world to share in her thoughts and feelings. She is married to Michael and the person she would most like to meet is Bono, the lead singer of U2. "I would like to tell him that he should never stop singing and point out that his songs have helped me to write so many poems."

CONVERSATION

And so again they met;
And talked, establishing their forms;
To soothe the eddies of such rising storms,
That cause the mind to fret.

Their spinning wheels of thoughts,
Can rub and slip; but then the rims adhere;
And for a time their minds together steer;
Their idle concentration caught.

But logic is a term for ordered frames,
That has its contradictions in its genes;
Without the real world no extra wisdom gleans;
Except for masters in their thinking games.

And so we climb, in thought, in twisting ways,
We search, combine, and phrases fast devise.
Our alternating thoughts attain the rise,
And on those levels set our minds to laze.

Reflections, with the swells of tension laid,
We find our rutted errors in hasty steps of mind,
Our after-wishes hope that past assertions trade
For better thoughts to tread and arguments to find.

John Armstrong, Loggerheads, Shropshire

SUMMERS PAST

Summer days
Are strewn through memory
Like glittering gemstones
In a stream
Too deep for reaching.

Moments of summer day
Are strung like beads,
Each in itself a jewel
Of many facets,
Radiating light -

Moments of morning when the sun
Filters through drifting mist
On fields of flowering grass;
Moments of golden afternoon,
And evening skies aflame.

Summers past
Lie in the depths of mind
Like a bright necklace,
Broken and scattered
On an ocean floor.

Dorothy Buyers, Oswestry, Shropshire

WAITING

I'm waiting for my boat to come in
I'm waiting for my children to ring.

I'm waiting for a beautiful lover
I'm waiting for something or other.

I'm waiting for the total eclipse
I'm waiting to feel someone's lips.

I'm waiting to feel sunshine on my face
I'm waiting to slow down the pace.

When I stop waiting will I die?
Or will I be waiting on the other side?

Susan Oakes, Clungunford, Shropshire

LOVE

Love can be warm and wonderful,
It can also be so cold.
Love can make your heart sing,
If there's someone there to hold.

Love should be freely given,
With a heart that's true.
Love can be so special,
Like the love I give to you.

Love's supposed to conquer all,
So the songs have said for years,
Love should bring you happiness,
But for me it brings more tears.

Christina Richards, Shrewsbury, Shropshire

LONGING

It's you I love,
I love no other;
You gave me children
Not another.

You gave me sorrow and many tears,
You gave me companionship through the years.
Now you are gone.

The time has passed
And I look back, as through a glass,
At our life together, and wonder whether
The succession of events suffered then
Would have been too much to bear apart.

Apart sounds unbearable,
But now you are no more,
And we are apart.

Jan Merrifield, Oswestry, Shropshire

A KING CHARLES

A King Charles is small and sweet,
he sits obediently by your feet.
He jumps up on your knee and sits,
he wags his tail and its licky lick.

His face is cute and very small,
he's brown and white and very bright.
And when it's time to have a walk,
his lead comes out as if he could talk.

He likes his walks by the riverside
walks with his master with great pride.
The rabbits in the field run off,
the dog is Keo and he's the boss.

Keo is a faithful friend,
he will not desert a true friend.
If in trouble he will stay,
by your side through night and day.

At night he sits upon her lap,
watching as you take a nap.
And when it's time to go to bed,
Keo says goodnight and bows his head.

Bill Williams, Oswestry, Shropshire

THE DRIVING LESSON

The day began as normal, the afternoon planned with a
drive
Out on a driving lesson, the friends sat side by side.
The test was due tomorrow, they drove through a busy
estate,
The car hit a very large pothole, what followed was all down
to fate.
Flames burst from under the bonnet, panic from inside the
car,
They both got out very quickly, leaving the car door ajar.
With a bus in the path of the fireball, back to the hand-
brake they sped,
They pulled it on tightly then hurried, to the telephone box
just ahead.
The firemen extinguished the car fire, an ambulance came
to the scene,
Another wailing siren, it seemed like horrible dream.
They hurriedly entered the flatlets, rescued the lady found
there,
She'd noticed the fire through the window, slipped and fell
on the stair.
Although she never recovered, the driver would never for-
get,
That traumatic lesson taken, before the successful test.

Joan Griffiths, Broseley, Shropshire

SHATTERED

This morning I awoke
a strong person
ready to face the world
on my terms.

But the world wasn't listening
it had promised me
so much, but it had lied.

The evening brought laughter
which soon
turned to tears
I shared with you.

You dropped the past
from a great height,
and it shattered indiscriminately
my jaded heart

Careful,
you tread on
the shards of my heart,
and risk cutting
your feet on my dreams.

Tracie M Jones, Shrewsbury, Shropshire

*Dedicated to Nathan, for the inspiration and the unfaltering
faith in me.*

THE PUNSTER

It's the lowest form of humour
Was once said of the old pun.
But the thing has been so popular
Since talking first begun.

The words that are the homophones
Are used by clever folk.
They also use the homonym
To make a pointed joke.

But the critics, they use sarcasm
Their comments are quite terse.
And prose is never so bad
That it can't be beat by verse.

Though some say the pun is bad;
And sarcasm is worse.
We all know that bad prose is bad;
Bad verse is even verse.

Frank Bramley, Telford, Shropshire

TRAPPED SPIRIT

Would anyone notice, would anyone care
If they came home one day, and I wasn't there?

Would they know where to look, have a clue where to start?
Or are they oblivious, to what goes on in my heart?

To walk beside streams, feel the earth beneath my feet
Roam the hills and dales, wild strawberries to eat.

Feel the rain on my face and the wind in my hair
Oh how much I long, to be living out there.

Birds and the animals, my faithful friends
A bed made of bracken, when each day ends.

Like the Romany roam, with no ties to bind me
The countryside my home, at last I'd be free.

Ann Chadwick, Bridgnorth, Shropshire

DREAMS

Castles of fantasy, built on hope
Dreams of love, established on trust,
Lightness of spirit, begins with touch
The one thing in common is the heart.

Amanda Gillies, St George's, Shropshire

LEARNING

I am only just learning
The things I need to know

I am only just learning
The way I need to go

I am only just learning
The seed I need to sow

I am only just learning
The way in which to grow

Through the Lord
I will be whiter than the snow
Because He loves me
This much I know

Daniel Ridgway, Wem, Shropshire

THE SAVING STORM

The storm arrived around midday,
Its harbinger a rushing breeze;
Directing branch and leaf to sway
In salutation on the trees.

Torn open as they skidded low,
The swollen, jostling clouds unfurled
In hissing, showering, shafting flow
To drumming union with the world.

And in the sting of slanting rain
Which briefly bounced and kicked up dust,
I laughed and washed away the pain
Of dying crops and how I'd cussed.

Oppressed by scorching sun and drought,
The storm lashed plants were further bruised.
They drank, as drenched and jerked about -
The providential gift well used.

At night, at rest, content once more
As shaken, showering droplets fell.
I listened to the river roar;
Relieved there'd be a crop to sell.

William Pyle, Whitchurch, Shropshire

William Pyle said: "I was born in Hertfordshire and emigrated at the age of 17 to Southern Rhodesia. Arriving in 1956, with five pounds in my pocket as a tobacco farming pupil, I progressed into farming for myself. 'The Saving Storm' recalls my farm in Zambia's Mkushi district. After 22 years in Africa I returned to a busy life in Britain, and am now enjoying time to write. I have a novel in progress. My love of poetry began as a schoolboy when introduced to the war poets. I have been married to Janet for 34 years and have three children and two grandchildren."

MY LITTLE PUPPY POLLY

My little puppy Polly can be naughty at times,
She runs around the garden in a great big whine,
Making lots of noise when the neighbours pass by,
Racing to the garden gate with a great big cry,
But I love my puppy Polly and that I
Just can't deny.

Samantha Johnson, Dudley, Staffordshire

THE SEASON OF SPRING

Snowdrops choke the winter shroud
Pansies cluster in a crowd

Lambs bound frantically in the green
Everywhere glistens with a springtime sheen

Now we have a misty dawn
Gone is winter's frosty morn

Fresh green shoots burst from the earth
Unchristened from their springtime birth

Sunshine shimmers on harvested field
As springtime casts its sparkling shield

Swallows skim across the sky
As the gentle breeze blows by

Glossy buds are all around
Snow is scarce upon the ground

No more storms of rushing rain
Winter's scared to show again

Heidi Charlotte Brittlebank, Stafford, Staffordshire

A WEDDING DAY WISH

For a very special couple
on your very special day.
Let your married life together
be complete in every way.
As you follow all the footpaths
there will be some rocky roads.
Just be there for one another
and share those heavy loads.
For with every single bad time
comes a handful of the good,
And with love and understanding
you'll avoid the gloomy wood.
Your path will be a bright one,
through meadows lush and green.
So here's to your life together
you'll achieve your finest dream.

Cheryl Hulme, Stoke-on-Trent, Staffordshire

A LOVELESS WORLD

Let me be free, let me go,
let me escape from this life you'll never know,
How I long to fly away,
I slowly suffocate every day,
trapped in here never to see,
what life would be like if I had the key,
to a world with real love and perfection,
for the earth has been sucked dry of true affection.
I think about this shell of living,
I begin sieving
through an eternity of memories to find,
those few who have been loving and kind,
So for now I am to stay
first where I am but soon I may
just fly away.
I don't need wings, I don't need feathers just
a heart full of love is a must,
to set me free
Forever!

Cara Beckett, Stoke, Staffordshire

MY LITTLE ANGEL

I saw a twinkle in a child's eye today
And all of my troubles just drifted away.

A smile a giggle and out came the sun.
A tickle and peep-po we did have such fun.

At the end of the day when sleepy eyes slept.
The joy of her little head tucked in my neck.

I looked at the joy and contentment on a little mite's face.
Another welcome addition to greet the human race.

Wendy Simons, Tamworth, Staffordshire

Dedicated to Sam, Lewis and my little angel, Hope xx.

WOLF

Sharp fangs sparkle
In the moonlight
A shrill and eerie howl
Stirs the silent night.

Springing into action
Dodging all the trees,
Moving with the darkness
Hoping no one sees.

He's an expert at pouncing
At hunting he is good
He's not afraid of anything,
Except Miss Riding Hood.

Lois Olivia Cooper, Newcastle, Staffordshire

RIDING A RAINBOW

Please catch me a rainbow if you can.
Bring me its colours and its hues
So I may ride it whilst it lasts.
Be lost in its changing shades
And feel its colours touch my skin
To charge my spirit and give me hope.

Margaret Kaye, Stafford, Staffordshire

Born in Leicester **Margaret Kaye** enjoys writing, painting,
drawing and gardening. "I started writing when I was diag-
nosed with ME six years ago," she explained. "I joined the
ME poetry group to raise money for research into this
bizarre illness. My work is influenced by my own life and
my style is both serious and humorous." Margaret is a
retired personal assistant with an ambition to keep writing
poetry. She is widowed and has one son, Mark. "I have
written short stories as well as a large number of poems
and I have produced two books," she said. "The person I
would most like to meet is Nelson Mandela because of his
patience, charm and bravery against all odds."

THE MUSEUM

Dimly lit, so quiet, so cold
The twilight zone.
The air shivers, sighing a thousand breaths
Monumental, so quiet, so old.

Shadows flicker in the half-light
Fleeting silver outlines against a haze of gold
The atmosphere is tangible
With the bitter-sweet tears of history.

Trapped in time.
Beauty preserved forever
Mist behind the thick glass cases.
Untouched but not unloved.

Thousands of visitors, yet few linger. The lights go out.
Far away, an oak door slams
Yet still they wait,
For the day when sweet sunlight will envelop them.

Patient, unmoving in their thankless task.
The overseers of humanity,
Yet not a flicker of resentment crosses their gleaming faces.
Eternal, as we are, for as long as we are.

Charlotte Merry, Tamworth, Staffordshire

Charlotte Merry said: "I have been writing for many years, and I often use poetry as a form of expressing my innermost feelings and emotions. Many writers and poets have influenced my work, but the poet I admire most is Carol Ann Dutry. My friends, family and previous English teacher, Mrs O'Leary support and encourage my writing ambition. I aspire to be a writer or a poet, someone who will be remembered in the future. In my spare time, my two main occupations are reading and writing. I am the Editor of my school newspaper and a participant in the Duke of Edinburgh award."

VALENTINE'S DAY

My lover's so sloppy and he shows it all the while
Even when I'm down he kisses me with a smile
He buys me lots of Galaxy chocolate and he buys me funky
flowers.
And he tantalises me, with his love powers
He sends me cards at Christmas and presents
when I'm unwell,
Whenever we go out, he always rings my bell
He surprises me with gold celtic-styled rings,
He knows I like gold jewellery and all the expensive things
I love you, so very much and I try to show it every minute of
the day,
And so let's hope, we're the perfect match
And we never slip away.

Kerry Beeston, Cannock, Staffordshire

DON'T LET THE PAST HAUNT YOU

Don't let the past haunt you
Let your soul be free.
Begin your life, live again,
Give your heart to me.

I'll take care not to break it,
So softly I'll tread.
For I have fallen so deeply
My heart rules my head.

I'll soothe your pain.
I'll ease your mind
I'll kiss away your fears.
Don't let the hurt that someone did
Take all of your best years.

Jane Armstrong, Burton-upon-Trent, Staffordshire

A PAGAN PLACE

Listen, you disbelievers, do not scoff and turn your face
There is power held in wood and stone within this pagan
place.
Just lay your hands on this cold stone.
Potency of time locked in its heart.
Or hear the mighty oak tree moan.
Winter wind thrashed in the dark.
This moor has seen eight thousand years
And will see a thousand more.
Though blasted cold by winter's tears,
Frost hard, to spring's cold thaw.
This is a place of hills and sky
Where only the hardy roam.
With bogs and heath, where the ravens fly.
Over wandering sheep, and the lonely shepherd's home.
This never was a place for foolish man to dwell.
A lonely place, a mystic place, caught in a pagan spell.

John Pegg, Meir, Staffordshire

John Pegg said: "This poem is one of my personal
favourites, reflecting the atmosphere of the Staffordshire
Moorlands. I commenced writing poetry three years ago.
Since then I have written over 400. This is my 30th to
appear in an anthology. I have also had two collections
printed privately after friends had requested me to do so. A
third collection is to be published around Christmas 2002
to be called 'Yuletide Shadows' (A Gallery of Ghosts). For
further details write to me, John Pegg, 1175 Uttoxeter
Road, Meir, Staffs, ST3 6HJ."

LISTS FOR LIFE

Things to achieve before I die,
To help make me smile, laugh and cry,
Enjoy life, be happy, have loads of fun,
Meet someone to love, a gorgeous Hun.

Lose excess weight become happy and thin,
Find real friends; throw fake uns in bin
Get a decent job, in the career of my choice,
Learn to open up, let people hear my voice.

Write some love stories, get published a few books,
Get people to judge me on what's inside not looks
Finally I must inherit the ability to love,
And become a free spirit, like a sole white dove.

Jane Johns, Cannock, Staffordshire

A COUNTRY SUMMER

Summer is upon us once more,
The sweet smell of flowers when
You open the door.

The countryside smells clean and fresh,
Animals they come out to play
During the month of May.

A time for picnics galore,
Families they always return for more.

Flowing by the riverside,
Are narrowboats giving rides.

Birds they chirp a cheery song
All through the summer long.

Nicola Regan, Stoke-on-Trent, Staffordshire

A GEM IN THE IRISH SEA

On top of South Stack, Anglesey, as we've ne'er seen before
The rushing mist envelope the sea, the gulls unable to
soar.
The horn of the lighthouse every few seconds is sounding.
The land is being covered and the waves are not pounding.

By afternoon it's finished its journey far from Ireland across
the sea,
The blue sky has appeared and views all around are again
visible as it's meant to be.
For peace and tranquillity definitely visit South Stack,
I would go any day and be glad to be back.

M Baxter, Uttoxeter, Staffordshire

HIS LOVE

He wooed his dearest love with nosegays rare,
He serenaded her with song and rhyme.
Her glorious hair, perfumed by sweet wild thyme,
Caressed the milk-white shoulders, wondrous fair.
He wove for her a primrose coronet
To wear while dancing on the dew-kissed lawn,
Until the rosy light of early morn.
Revealed a glade, deep strewn with violet.

Into a fragrant honeysuckle bower
He took his love one sultry afternoon,
And kissed her rosy lips and hazel eyes.
She lay, contented, till a sudden shower
Persuaded her to shelter far too soon,
Behind the cat-flap, where her basket lies.

Shirley Price, Haughton, Staffordshire

MY LOVE

My love she is my life, my opposite, my right from wrong.
She is my belief in doubt, my truth in the midst of lies.
My love she is aesthetic coefficient, my beauty to my beast.
A treasure to behold

Always and ever my love exudes true life behind all that is
pleasing to the eyes of the soul.
Such love and beautiful love can be yours and mine if only
we can believe.

Kenneth Ginders, Stoke-on-Trent, Staffordshire

TRUE FRIENDSHIP

A true friend is quite rare,
but when you find one they'll always be there,
a true friend will be there through all, good and bad,
a true friend will be there when you're happy and when
you're sad,
a true friend is someone to share your deepest secrets with,
a true friend is there when your problems get too much
and you just don't want to live,
someone to help you live an enjoyable life to the full,
when you've got a true friend life is never dull,
when you're at school a friend's just there to help you have
fun,
but when you're older and you lose contact, you miss all
the things you've done,
a true friend is there for life, and not just a short time,
so keep in touch, then you won't pine.

Stephanie Abberley, Stoke-on-Trent, Staffordshire

TULIPS

One morning, I awoke
And found that the world was full of tulips.
Colours, pure like friendship,
And vivid like new life
Swam past me and through me
Spinning like paint in a washing machine.

I rose from the clawing winter
Where Christmas trees loomed like angry giants
And the icy rain, blood-red like a valentine,
Left scars on my mind and on my arm.
It writhed and swirled, a tormented fog
That lifted, and I could breath again.

I pick a stray tulip, lost in a sea of sunshine
So soft, so delicate, so beautiful.
New love reflects in its fresh green leaves.
The golden laughter of old friends warms the air
And spring opens up her arms to me,
Healing.

Rose Starkie, Weston, Staffordshire

For Vivienne Starkie, my mum.

WHY?

Deeply hurt
Cannot cry
Accusations
Don't know why

Cannot love
If cannot trust
Love we knew
Now turned to dust

Sunken hearts
Shallow eyes
Shattered dreams
Our love goodbye

Ian Challinor, Stafford, Staffordshire

ASLEEP OR AWAKE

I sometimes watch you as you sleep,
your face in my mind I'll always keep.
I know one day that you won't wake
but you'll be there my thoughts to take.

In the still of the night I feel so calm
as the silence soothes me like a balm.
When morning comes, the world's awake
of my dream what will I make?

Was I awake or was I dreaming,
have my thoughts got a meaning?
The only thing I really know
asleep or awake, I love you so.

Catherine Lambert, Stoke-on-Trent, Staffordshire

REALITY OR FANTASY

Bewitched by his piercing gaze,
An Italian stallion half my age,
Arouses a deep passion with rage.

The rainbow flame of desire lights,
On this sensual provocative night,
Body language signals delight.

Arousing touches, face to face,
Affectionate kisses, thrusting embrace,
Funny I don't feel any disgrace.

Jackie O'Nions, Burntwood, Staffordshire

THE BIRDS AND THE BEES

The stork drops off,
Then rings the doorbell,
Runs half a mile,
Because of the smell,
The nappy needs changing,
There's food to be bought,
So much work because of the stork,
But as they grow up they learn to use their mouths,
More, more they shout and they shout,
When school comes round,
You jump for joy,
As there's peace and quiet for you to enjoy,
But you forget they'll be back at half past three,
Shouting where's my tea where's my tea,
Don't forget the worst is still to come,
The teenage years are just over the hump,
They argue they shout out till all hours of the night,
Then you wish they were a little mite.

Andrea Haynes, Hednesford, Staffordshire

THE WILLOW GROVE

In summertime I make my way, footsteps hushed on mossy
path,
Towards the ancient willow tree whose magic casts a spell on
me.

Its branches old and gnarled sweep down, a living curtain giv-
ing shade.
A special place, where I'll find rest, from daily toil and mental
stress.

I slip between the swaying fronds; the grass is soft beneath my
feet.
Green light blends with misty mauve in my garden room, the
willow grove.

The rustic arbour beckons me, built long ago by loving hands,
A sturdy frame where eglantine, and clematis, and rose
entwine.

Sunbeams glint through trembling leaves, reflecting on the
glassy pond.
Make dappled patterns all around this secret place that I have
found.

The trilling thrush, the humming bees, is all the company I
need
As I recline on woven seat, to dream awhile in my retreat.

Maureen Edden, Tamworth, Staffordshire

Maureen Edden said: "Two years ago I joined a writers' group and
tentatively began to write short stories, before progressing to poetry.
It took some time for me to find my own style. Suddenly I found
amazing and beautiful images running around in my head. My first
poems virtually wrote themselves. I owe much of my success to my
husband and the members of my group for their encouragement and
critiques. I am a retired teacher, married with four grown-up chil-
dren. I am an avid reader. I am also passionate about gardening and
visiting places of natural beauty. Extensive travel around Europe
and the UK have had a strong influence on my work."

HOMECOMING

Home to the washing the dishes the chores
Shinning the brasses wiping the doors.
The windows are dirty the garden unkempt,
The paths and the steps have never been swept.
Home is the traveller home from the sea.
I'm supposed to be happy. So what's wrong with me?
Home's where the heart is the poets all say,
If I win the lottery, I'm off and away.
I'll be the traveller, that'll be me.
Back to the long road and back to the sea.

Ethel May Hatfield, Stoke-on-Trent, Staffordshire

THE NEW BABY

Mother says I mustn't touch,
I don't know as I want to much.
It doesn't walk or talk or run.
It does not do much at all.
Before it came it was to be
A real friend to be with me.
(I have been so alone you know)
I'm told in time that it will grow
But quite how fast I just don't know,
For now it seems a little slow
At learning who I am and what
It merely lies and cries a lot.
I think I'll ask it to go back,
Its changing mat I'll even pack!
In exchange I'll have a bike,
Or something else I really like.
Whatever I have it will be
Better fun that mom's baby.

Pamela Dyke, Wombourne, Staffordshire

MY BEAUTIFUL DAUGHTER

My beautiful daughter
You cannot know
How much my heart breaks
As I watch you grow

In time you'll become
Independent and free
Always my daughter
And special to me

As you grow older
You will see
Through the eyes of a mother
Reflections of me

Past, present and future
All intertwined
My mother, your mother
All daughters you'll find

Our reflections, not vanity
Mirrored lives we share
Always a daughter
Your mother, who cares.

Julie Copeland, Fenton, Staffordshire

SEVENTIETH BIRTHDAY

You've reached your three score years and ten,
And twenty will not come again,
Make the most of every day,
Do not whittle time away.

Enjoy your life as best you can,
With family, friends, just everyone,
But give yourself some time to stare
At nature's gifts - they're all out there.

So, happy days for you, and more -
Another year, no, another score.

Joyce Thorley, Stoke-on-Trent, Staffordshire

UPON A CLIFFTOP

In beds of contoured folds the weathered limestones lie
With grey-veined fields and rough, stone walls.
An arid tor cocks its nose to the southern sky,
To darkness and those nearing squalls.

Below, eager crabbers, staple-like, search and probe
In flooded crevice or overhang,
Where brown oarweed waves its long-tongued lobes
And the mournful note of the buoy goes clang.

At the ebb of the tide the churning water returns
Sweeping the platform that we used to see.
Now crabbers move homeward between gorse and the ferns
Leaving those clinted cliffs to wild rabbits and to me.

Jenkyn Evans, Wombourne, Staffordshire

PRECIOUS TIME

Time waits for no one, oh, how time flies,
Time is so precious,
These words are uttered every day,
No time to gaze at the moon above,
Or smell the new-mown hay,
No time to laugh,
No time to cry,
No time to love,
No time to pray, in the old stone church,
On the seventh day.
"Wherever does time go?" we sigh,
As we live our busy lives,
Busy as bumble bees,
In honey hives.
No time to dance,
No time to sing,
No time to paint or write sweet poetry,
No time to chase the end of a rainbow,
No time to sit and dream.

Dorothy Chadwick, Stoke-on-Trent, Staffordshire

Dorothy Chadwick said: "I was inspired to write poetry on
September 11th 2001, when the terrible events took place
in New York. I wrote a poem about the tragedy. I have had
many poems published in hardback books and several in
my local newspaper. I live with my partner, Stuart in the
beautiful Staffordshire moorlands. I enjoy caravanning, the
countryside, and visiting places of national and historical
interest. I am also a steam train enthusiast. I hope to pub-
lish a book of poetry for children in the near future."

CATS-CRADLE ON THE WWW

Every twelve minutes
Someone gets angry with their mouse.
Tangled up in the internet,
Going round the houses.
I used to play cats-cradle with wool,
Now I play it with search engines,
Google, Alta Vista, Yahoo, Scoot2,
Scoot2 where?
Click, search, wait,
Wait, double click,
Oh sod it.

Frances Matten, Stoke-on-Trent, Staffordshire

THE EMPTY HOUSE

Dark, dusty furniture fills the room,
Partly-closed curtains add to the gloom,
Silence descends like a blanket of cloud,
No childish laughter or music played loud.
No voices raised in anger and pain,
Just the dull roar of the wind and the rain.
The man sits unmoving, unshaven and pale,
Unseeing eyes stare at yesterday's mail.
Hands clasped together as if in deep prayer,
Forgotten cigarette burns a hole in the chair.
The house is empty, though he's sitting there.
His family have gone. He doesn't know where.

Sylvia Dodds, Stoke-on-Trent, Staffordshire

THE AUTUMN SPINNER

Silently spinning he works through the night
With only the moon to give him light.
He makes not a sound as he spins with his thread,
Performing a miracle while we are in bed.

When I wake in the morning and open my door,
I'll gaze at the miracle performed in the night, once more.
For the trees he has changed with his mysterious webs,
And the dew that has fallen gives lustre to his wonderful
threads.

Joan Wilde, Lichfield, Staffordshire

THE ARRIVAL

The sun gleamed on steep majestic hills
Snowdrops glistened softening February chills
Spring began to glimpse the air
A wonderful freshness everywhere
The gentle breeze caressed the dale
All our yesterdays began to pale
From the bridge the River Dove
Splashed its jewels of continuous love
A new beginning another day
The joy of life had come my way

Linda Timmis, Newcastle-under-Lyme, Staffordshire

THE TRUE GIFT OF LOVE

When I am alone, no TV, no phone,
Just a ticking of the clock,
My thoughts turn to our love.

A sleeping babe is proof of this,
No worries has she, just joy and bliss.
Your kindness and love through her veins flow,
Your soul encapsulated, just waiting to grow.
Such a wonder is she, your perfect gift to me,
A gift we can share for eternity.
Words cannot express my love for you now.
All I know is every day you give it space to grow.

Joanne Rainbow, Alrewas, Burton-upon-Trent, Staffordshire

Born in the West Midlands **Joanne Rainbow** has interests
including playing the organ and walking on the routes of
old railway lines. "I have always written poetry especially at
low and high points in my life," she remarked. "My greatest
inspiration is my husband whom I met whilst working in
the railway industry. My style comes straight from the
heart and I would like to be remembered just as I am, with
no airs and graces." Aged 29, Joanne is a housewife with
an ambition to live a long and happy life. She is married to
Gary and they have one daughter, Molly. "As well as short
stories I have written hundreds of poems," said Joanne.
"The people I would most like to meet are Elton John and
Bernie Taupin. It makes my spine tingle to think what a
great artistic combination they are."

VAMPIRES

Shells of human and thirst for blood,
Are vampires necessarily bad or good?
That's the world constantly wanting to classify,
Sometimes for no apparent reason why.
They only age in wisdom and never die,
Is that the truth or do you wonder why?

Melanie Louise Heath, Stoke-on-Trent, Staffordshire

IMAGES VI

Thou fledst from me that sometime did me seek
And took with thee the balm that sooth'd my wounds
The tortur'd axis of a mind too weak
Convuls'd without thee in the sunless noons.

But day by day with each new practis'd skill,
I sens'd the nature of my love for thee;
Yet nurs'd a melancholy yearning still
Which thy sweet presence can alone set free.

As moth, toward the dazzling light still drawn,
And flutt'ring in unseemly panic die:
My sacrifice to thee and children born
Who journey freely in a cloudless sky.

Lo, thus, in ecstasy, despair and pain,
My distillated passion starved again.

Victor Church, Stratford-upon-Avon, Warwickshire

WINTER

Reynard was dying by the cruel whip.
He shivered but the red blood still fell.
The cracking of the branches was
Made by the sound of the
Hooves of the huntsman's horse.

The dark colour of the night gathered,
And sighing his last sigh, Reynard died.
As the galloping of the hooves
Fades into the darkness
The river creeps
And takes the dead fox away.

The bare forest falls,
Leaving the wild creatures
Hiding under the dead leaves of the ground.

Faarea Masud, Coventry, Warwickshire

Faarea Masud said: "I am 16, female, and have been
ridiculously passionate about writing ever since I wrote my
first story about a boot chasing a malteser when I was six.
Since then, I've had numerous publications in several liter-
ary magazines and anthologies, and hope to become a
world famous, internationally bestselling author worthy of
winning all the awards in the world, including the Nobel! I
also fancy myself to be the owner of The Times by the age
of 36. If not, then I'll settle for being a journalist for my
local paper. I've also written three novels."

TO BE A WEALTHY MAN

To pretend it doesn't matter
Is to say it won't get dark
It's easier without it, is a lie
To pretend there's no desire
To be a wealthy man
Is like saying
You don't mind what time you die
To pretend your life is easy
With no money in your bank
Is like flying in a plane
That has no wings
But, to pretend that you are happy
Could be true, for all I know
For there's beauty
In so many many things

Angela Corrall, Norton Lindsey, Warwickshire

Born in Bristol **Angela Corrall** has interests including antiques, playing league tennis, painting and writing. "I started writing poetry ten years ago during a very difficult time in my life," she remarked. "My work is influenced by nature and injustice of all kinds and my style is sad but honest. I would like to be remembered for putting the truth on paper and touching people's hearts." Angela is a former nurse with an ambition to have her own book of poems published, featuring the best of the 100 she has written. She is married to David and they have five children. "My biggest fantasy is to recite my poems on TV or radio," she said.

TRANSFORMATION

Gold on blue
A dragonfly flew,
Misty water merged;
Grey sky converged.
Gold on blue
Sunrise makes new.
Light changes all.
Hear the birds call
Gold on blue.

Kathryn Graham, Warwick, Warwickshire

MUSIC

Do you hear it? can you feel it?
Tingling through your mind,
Projecting your thoughts
Etching pictures and memories
People and places,
Time and history;
Your life glides by in a song.
A hit of the past, a slit of a thought,
And memories flow,
Cascading to the present,
And you are there in the past
You relive it, for three minutes,
The people, the places, the smells
The atmosphere, the sounds, the buildings;
All in notes.
And, if you're lucky, you will travel
To another destination
With the next tune
To begin again.

Rita Carter, Leamington Spa, Warwickshire

AUBURN

Sudden the glory burning before me,
Sun-captured crescendo of copper and bronze,
Rich rippling chestnut all glossy gold stroked,
Threaded with rubies the colour of blood.
In auburn's bright flame mahogany burns,
Mingling hot embers with red cedarwood,
And I, all amazed, gaze into the flare,
Entranced by the girl with the beautiful hair.

Pauline Brown, Warwick, Warwickshire

DEBBIE

I am a rock standing on solid ground
Tall, supportive and loving
To people around.

I take on people's troubles as if they were my own
I get worn down by it all sometimes
And can often feel alone.

Walking in the countryside makes me feel free and alive
Space is important to me
Allowing me to connect with my inner child.

I am a romantic soul at heart sensitive, serious and deep
To watch a sunset and sunrise
Makes me feel whole and complete.

Lately I've been soul-searching, who am I, what to do?
I can't see where I am going but my faith will get me
through
Who am I? Debbie.

Debbie McLeod, Nuneaton, Warwickshire

HE IS HERE

It doesn't matter if the cup you bring is empty
It doesn't matter if you feel that love's grown cold,
It makes no difference that your hopes have come to nothing
It makes no difference that you've passed this way before.

He is here to melt your heart again.
He is here to melt your heart again.

If all you have is a mind filled with confusion
And even now, you feel like you're alone.
There's no need to tell him of your failures.
There's no need to fear for what's to come.

He is here to fill your life again.
He is here to fill your life again.

Lyn Smailes, Warwick, Warwickshire

Born in London **Lyn Smailes** enjoys salsa dancing and gardening. "I started writing poetry at school," she remarked. "I was encouraged by some amazing English teachers. My work is influenced by my Christian faith, my friendships and the books I read and I would describe my style as personal and emotive. I would like to be remembered as someone who cared about people and the environment." Lyn is a part-time teacher and counsellor. She is married to Jeff and they have four children. "As well as poems I have written several songs," she said. "My biggest fantasy at the moment is to get personal tuition from a salsa champion!"

GRANDAD

What is man that he should die like this
Barely animal, deprived of dignity
Drained of knowledge and humility?

What is God that He should treat men so
Gnawed hollow from the inside out
Burning within, faded with doubt?

What is the body when the soul has gone
When flame has died and the purpose fled
Scarcely alive, most nearly dead?

What is grandad now but memory
A tear, a dream, a broken thought
Lost in pain and burned to nought?

Emma Melville, Nuneaton, Warwickshire

Born in Ipswich **Emma Melville** has interests including, fantasy, ancient history, Celtic tradition, folk music and dancing. "I started writing poetry at secondary school and my work is influenced by folk music, fantasy, myth and my own feelings," she explained. "My style is more lyric than poetry and my ambition is to publish a book of my work." Aged 30, she is a teacher. She is married to Jon and they have children Toby and Hazel. "As well as poems I have written short stories," she said. "My biggest fantasy is being rich enough to spend time writing instead of going to work."

WAITING ARMS

When trees upon the wind do blow,
And winter skies are filled with snow,
When icy rivers cease to flow,
May warm arms wait for you.

When all the ground is frozen hard
And flowers, all their leaves discard,
When all the fields are ploughed and scarred,
May soft arms comfort you.

When all the creatures hide away,
And icicles seem set to stay,
When Jack Frost on the land does play,
May kind arms care for you.

When all the world is cold and bleak,
And robins raise a hungry beak,
When in the cold you're feeling weak,
May strong arms carry you.

And when the winter's far away,
And sunshine fills a summer day,
Those arms, forgotten in your play,
Be always there for you.

Angela Dunsby, Shipston-on-Stour, Warwickshire

Born in Birmingham **Angela Dunsby** enjoys reading, music,
tennis and horse-riding. "I started writing poetry at school,"
she remarked. "English was the only subject I really enjoyed
and people seemed to enjoy my work and encouraged me. My
poetry is influenced by day-to-day events or feelings and I
would like to be remembered as honest and willing to try
almost anything." Aged 31, Angela is a housewife with an
ambition to publish her own book of poetry. She is married to
Matthew and they have children Luke and Mary. "The person I
would move like to meet is Elvis Presley because he is the king
of rock and roll," she said.

RUNAWAY

Run, run, into the night
Into the forest
Out of sight

Go, go away from them all
Do not return
And do not call

Run, run, until they have gone
You are their prey
You must go on.

Race, race do not make a din
Go far from here
And don't let them win

Run, run, into the night
You are not safe
Though they are not right

Quick, quick, they can't catch you now
They're not in control
You beat them somehow.

Becky Lucas, Bedworth, Warwickshire

Born in Nuneaton **Becky Lucas** enjoys writing songs and poetry as well as performing drama with a local theatre company. "I started writing poetry when I was very young," she explained. "I used to be quite shy and needed a form of expression but then continued writing poetry because I found it enjoyable. My work is influenced by everyday life and my personal feelings. I would describe my style as mellow. I would like to be remembered as someone who tried to do her best at everything she attempted." Aged 21, Becky has an ambition to be a well-known writer and performer. She and her partner, Ben, have one son, Rhys. "I have written many songs and stories as well as a large number of poems," she said. "The person I would most like to meet is Bryan Adams because his music has been my biggest influence."

WAITING

Waiting on a bench in the sun
Waiting.
Waiting for no one,
The wind teases me
I turn to see
Where it comes from.
And why are the leaves running,
Chasing circles around my bench?
They no more know why they run
Than I know why I wait.

Yve Smithers, Rugby, Warwickshire

CHOCOLATE BOX

Can anybody hear me?
Is anybody there?
I'm trapped inside a chocolate box with
truffles in my hair.
There's strawberry creams in my ears, there's
nougat on my nose.
There's Turkish delight and caramel wedged
between my toes.
I'm trying to stick to my diet, there's orange
creams at my finger tips.
I know a moment in the mouth is a lifetime on
the hips.
Can someone come and rescue me, please remove
this coffee cream.
Then I woke up with a startle, thank God it was
just a dream.

Margaret Power Burnip, Nuneaton, Warwickshire

FORCES OF NATURE

The forces of nature still reign
In volcano and hurricane
With wings swept back
The roaring jet
Invades the vast expanse of sky
To claim its superiority.
On land the tilting train
Leaves its name on negotiated bends with speed,
Yet still we lack the willingness to tame
Our environment for more than desires of greed.

Pat Bidmead, Nuneaton, Warwickshire

HAIKAI

Twixt satanic malls
tall billboards hiding green trees
that ain't there no more.

Goulash of people
swilling, grubbing fast food for
collective stomachs.

Suburban welking
few birds still perching forlorn
on TV gallows.

Go south, north or west
young man, wave at Dantesque
fellows, damned souls.

Anthony Emberger-Hughes, Long Compton, Warwickshire

MAN OF WORDS (A TRIBUTE TO JOHN BETJEMAN)

He wore a worn and worsted waistcoat,
With crumpled collar and natty tie,
Cigarette in holder,
Books and banded boater to finish off.

He was a man of word,
Many words on railways, churches and
aspects of life in this our England.
Graphic word pictures, he painted,
for one and all to enjoy.

Christopher Smith, Birmingham, Warwickshire

TRUE FRIENDSHIP

To have true friendship
You don't need riches or fame;
Friendship is an understanding,
More than knowing a face or a name.

Holding out a loving hand
When things seem to go wrong;
Saying comforting words,
Making a weak heart strong.

A true friend
Will always be standing by,
To catch you if you fall,
To wipe your tears if you cry.

Whether in times of happiness
Or in the depth of despair,
A true friend
Will always be there.

Sue J Bell, Nuneaton, Warwickshire

SHORT LIFESPAN

Flung against a wall
Crying for attention
He lost his temper
She died of head injuries
Short lifespan, nine weeks

Shaken to death
Cold, hungry and alone
Beaten severely
Teeth knocked out
Short lifespan, two years

Months of brutal treatment
Perforated eardrum, cigarette burns
Lay dying on the sofa
Then sex on the floor
Short lifespan, four years

Likely to be murdered
Before the first birthday
Than at any other time
Brief and tortured lives
Mankind's most hideous crime

Neil Phillips, Nuneaton, Warwickshire

FROZEN LOVE

Faint snowflakes cascade and brush the frozen floor,
And star-shaped remnants of autumn are covered once more.
The moon illuminates a manuscript so fine
With a library of thoughts on every line
The night lingers on, with ice in the air
And the frost that destroyed a perfect affair
The morning sun shows this love will not last
The years, but moments have now flown past.
The warmth filters through and gives a warm glow
For new feelings of love once more to bestow.

Victoria Brown, Nuneaton, Warwickshire

LUV

Gary loved Lucy will all his young heart;
He told her so, and they told one and all.
Furthermore, Gary indulged in his art,
Making a start with his local school wall:
"I luv U L" read his graffiti's scrawl.
He then defaced the village hall, the shop,
And the pub, in large letters six feet tall:
Enthused by some spray paint muse, until stopped.
When Lucy saw, and dropped him on the spot.
Gary was shocked, but said he did not care.
Then, late one night, he scrubbed the whole lot off;
But forgot his last gift: the watch she wears;
Heartfelt and hidden, the last of the list:
"Forever yours, Gaz" still kisses her wrist.

Simon Gunter, Rugby, Warwickshire

HAIKU: RUBICON

Two in the morning.
We walk in St James's Park
And over the bridge.

Alex Galloway, Kenilworth, Warwickshire

EXPERIENCE

The school of life is always open,
so that folk may learn each day.
of all the things that make life's pattern
in black or white or shades of grey.

Of things that make one's life worth living,
like helping others on their way.
A friendly word, a kindly deed
may help to make somebody's day.

The teacher is experience
and that makes the foolish wise.
The lessons sometimes hard to learn
are but blessings in disguise.

For as we walk the corridors
of life from day to day
and come to grips with all the things
that fate can throw our way,
we call upon experience to show us what to do
and if we've learnt the lessons right
then they should see us through.

John Arnold, Coleshill, Warwickshire

A TOOTH

There is a very small tooth
In a very small mouth
It is now coming loose and soon will fall out

It will leave a small gap not very wide
But a new tooth is coming
Though it's still trying to hide

It's not all that sad
Yes he's filled with delight
For he'll put that old tooth under his pillow tonight

The fairy will come
And whisk it away
There in its place some pennies she'll lay

In a casket she'll place it and carry it home
Then she will give it
To the chief garden gnome

He'll polish and scrub it to make it all clean
Then he'll deliver it
To the tooth fairy queen

Paul Kelly, Atherstone, Warwickshire

DARK CREEK

Silent and still.
A cloak of whispering darkness,
shrouds and engulfs in an encompassing claustrophobic
cocoon.
Silence, broken by ripples,
of luminous silver, grey-green phosphorescence.
As the tide returns to the steeply-sided wooded creek,
valley sides echo with the haunting, baying bark of a dog
fox.
Rising silently, a rich bright yellow golden glow,
splits the night, breaking land from sky and earth from
water.
Casting shadows from ancient gnarled twisted oaks,
in an eerie silhouette shadows twist and turn,
in a spiralling gyrating ghost dance across the rippling tide.
Reaching its zenith night moonlight shines in a cloudless
sky
as reflections sink beneath the dark shimmering waters.
Eddies of whistling breeze, stir the silence,
waiting for the sun and dawn
to warm the earth,
in commencement of another new day.

Howard Lucas, Stratford-on-Avon, Warwickshire

SPOCKIE

At the open window he sits looking out to sea,
ears twitching listening content
my silent feline friend, my confidant with
fur soft against my face whose heart
beats with mine.

What thoughts Spockie as you gaze
across the sand, do you see beyond
the horizon where the sun now rests, at
peace knowing your spirit is free behind
those eyes that now stare back at me?

Do you sense my pain, know
loneliness as I?
I sigh and stroke your coat of silk
that calms my restless spirit, appreciate
you understand my need of silence.

Sheila Rogers, Walsall, West Midlands

*Dedicated to Will, the artist whose painting of Spockie
inspired me to write down my thoughts. Also to those who
understand.*

Born in Darlaston **Sheila Rogers** enjoys writing, music and
painting in watercolours. "I started writing poetry when I
retired, to fulfil an ambition," explained Sheila. "My work is
influenced by life, compassion and music and my style is
open. I would like to be remembered with a smile." Aged 66,
Sheila is married to Ernest and they have two children,
Steve and Dave, as well as two grandsons, Tom and Callum.
"I have had some of my short stories published and some of
my poems have been put into print," said Sheila. "My
biggest fantasy is be asked to sign my bestselling novel and
to be recognised by my peers," she said. "My worst night-
mare is having my house invaded by frogs."

HERITAGE 2002

Red
Bloodied crusaders and soldiers still fighting.
Poppies in silent vigil over the fallen
Attack and defence, England team shirts
All giving themselves for victory.

White
Smooth skin of infancy, slowly maturing
Scarred and mottled with pride and acceptance
Cliffs of Dover beckoning home
To freedom, innovation peace and hope.

Blue
Blood in the veins mixed with Commonwealth colours.
Birds over the cliffs of a distant refrain,
Skies on a perfect summer's day picnic.
Horizons calling to fresh opportunities.

Red, white, blue
Uniting a kingdom, river of jubilee flooding the Mall.
Respite from persecution and fear
Revealing a nation, Great...
Britain.

Carole Hare, Solihull, West Midlands

In memory of a selfless mother, Phyllis Hopkins, whose unfulfilled dream was to write stories in a rose-covered cottage.

Carole Hare said: "My poetry, written sporadically over nine years, is usually produced as a gift for family or friends on special occasions, including weddings and retirements. I like to incorporate some personal history of the recipient, often laced with humour. I find it important to look for laughter and hope in everyday situations, capturing unique and special memories in light-hearted verse. My mother passed on her love of books and reading, which we have encouraged in our own four children. My husband, Mike, jokes that I even read the backs of bus tickets. 'Heritage 2002' is my first poem to be published."

RESTLESSNESS

Turn on the light
Open your eyes
Smell the coffee
Taste the rain
Feel the breeze

He loves you,
He loves you not.

Turn out the light
Close your eyes
Dream a dream
Try to sleep

He loves you,
You love him not.

Mayumi Rosalynd Tew, Solihull, West Midlands

THE DESERTION

A world of peace was collapsing in sin,
With a bitter light of suffering about to begin.
As the sky opened up and let out a wild cry,
A bolt of blue lightning crashed out of its eye.
It twisted and turned through the bracken and haze,
Spiralling through the jungle as the branches forged a
maze.
The desert it skid past like a whirlwind of fire,
By the soft wheezing horses that roam on the mire.
Till the cities it filled from the head to the toe,
And the people were faced with disastrous woe.
Then the sky, it closed up as if it all was a dream,
And the sender of lightning was never again seen.

Faye Williams, Dudley, West Midlands

Faye Williams said: "I am currently studying for A-levels in
biology, Japanese, geography and maths. I have always
enjoyed creative writing and poetry but often I don't have
much time, so most of my work is written while I am on the
bus, reflecting on my day. Apart from creative writing, in
my free-time I also enjoy modern competitive disco dancing,
working part-time at boarding kennels and staying at home
cooking with my mom."

HAPPINESS

Happiness we cannot keep
to ourselves alone,
Joy is magnified when shared
with another one.
Laughing lips and sparkling eyes
Pass our pleasure on.
Brighten every path we tread
Bid dull care be gone.
May we always share our joys,
May each day begun
Help us lighten others' eyes
With delighted fun.

Jean Russell, Solihull, West Midlands

THE MOST COVETED GIFT

After being struck down by cancer in 1982

I found myself introspective about life and the meaning of
it.
Was it the last stroke of the dice?

Fortunately I survived by the skin of my teeth

Cometh the hour of our ruby wedding celebration

A lovely rainbow came out with colours - ruby red,
Amethyst, azure, gold, what a lucky omen

The look on my dear wife's face, it was like falling in love
All over again

A sharp reminder she remains the anchor of my life.

John Jenkins, Walsall, West Midlands

THE WHALE SONG

Every evening I sit on the dock
Every evening at six o'clock
The sun is setting, the ocean calm
Dandelion seeds float into my palm

But in the distance a sound can be heard
But it's not a shout or a tweet of a bird

A gentle humming, the song of a whale
The shimmer of spray and a glistening tail

And every evening the song is new
And I listen with pleasure
Wouldn't you?

Laura Castree, Wolverhampton, West Midlands

CHANGES

The heart ripped out of industry
Longbridge all but gone
City of million trades
Now down to one hundred and one,
Fast food and services
No need for any skill,
Blacksmith, button and gunmaker,
Estate agent now move in to kill.
Jewellery Quarter just holds it own
Cobblers have all but gone,
And as for the bookbinders,
I know of but one
Progress I hear you say,
Makes life better
But industry in the heart of Brum,
Has slowly passed away.

Thomas Blundell, Birmingham, West Midlands

BECKY IN BLUE

Her hair painstakingly braided, many a tear had been shed
it is true,
Until it conformed to her wishes, held tight by a scrunchie
of blue.
She strips off her shocking-pink track suit, joins the rest in
an orderly queue,
Her skinny white frame is embellished by her star-studded
leotard of blue.

The girls get into their warm up, their bodies like well-
tuned machines,
With stretching and bending and leaping, their fitness is
plain to be seen.
She silently follows the others, who giggle and chat as girls
do,
A picture of pure concentration, in her star-studded leotard
of blue.

There's Jodie and Megan and Lucy, Lauren, Nicola and
Fay,
They all have their own special talent, each performs in
their own unique way.
I go through each move with my Becky, as I watch from my
spectator's view,
I marvel at how she's progressing, that's my wonderful
Becky in blue.

Peter Hayling, Birmingham, West Midlands

DEADLY LESSONS

I wish maths hadn't any rules
Mainly they are made for fools
The numbers whiz around my head,
Maybe I should have stayed in bed.

English is another matter
My handwriting's all in a clatter,
Spelling the vocab has gone wrong
Why can't we just sing a song?

Science has never ever been worse,
Maybe I'm under a terrible curse
Chemistry, biology, physics galore,
Please, please say there is no more.

Hetvi Bhatt, Wolverhampton, West Midlands

GUILT

The reflection peers back from the mirror
The expression cool and grim,
A mask of innocence on the face,
That has to it no soul.

He stares, the reflection stares back,
Why do you stare so? am I evil? am I damned?
So was the sinister ritual he held after each unholy night.

The reflection gives no answers, but maddens him more,
Still he screams, still he gets no peace,
His soul shall remain restless,
Until he is caught,
And his sins are counted.

Kerry Smith, Wednesbury, West Midlands

SELF REFLECTION

In this dark cold lonely place,
my face is grey it's out of grace.
How did I get here I don't know, have I got much further to
go?
My strength is fading my heart is weak,
I don't seem to stand on my own two feet.
No one loves me no one cares,
I look around and there's no one there.
Who will free this soul of mine open the gate to love divine?
No one knows I'm locked away,
this happy face they see each day.
It's just a mask I always wear,
there's laughter lines and wrinkles there.
A giver to all this cloak I wear,
like a shroud it buries me,
ties me down and shackles me.
Someone soon must surely see, the me I am or yet to be.
In my darkness rescue me,
hear my call and fly to me.
Break these chains that bind me fast,
to the grey of all that's past.

Patricia Cousins, West Bromwich, West Midlands

DARK DAYS

Shadows were cast around the world,
When terror came out of the skies,
To attack the World Trade Center of America,
People's lives were lost,
How can we mend their ways?
Our peaceful lives betrayed,
Our enemies are scattered around the world,
We will battle to bring them to justice,
Give strength to our leaders who have a difficult task.

L Kelley, Birmingham, West Midlands

LONELINESS

Loneliness is a sad affair,
It's the one thing that everyone fears,
No one to share our problems with,
No one to help dry our tears.

No one to say when the answer is wrong,
No one to see us pass by,
No one to hear when we cry out for help,
No one to care when we die.

Living alone does not have to mean lonely,
All it takes is a wave or a call,
Just someone who'll say "hello" now and again,
Pick us up again each time we fall.

So if you know someone who's lonely
Someone in the depths of despair,
Stop by now and then, and just say hello,
Let them know that somebody does care.

Alan Davis, Walsall, West Midlands

THE SEASONS

Here comes Spring fair,
Brings lambs and foal mare.

Here comes Summer hot,
Butterfly, sunshine and apricot.

Here comes Autumn warm,
Now leaves fall and harvest is born.

Here comes Winter cruel,
Frost freezes river and pool.

Zoë Spencer, Sutton Coldfield, West Midlands

CIRCLES

Hair streaming in the wind,
I take my branch, I stoop down and
Trace circles in the sodden sand;
Deep spirals fill with brine.

I watch the eddies twirling by;
Nature's pattern echoes mine.
Flowers round, by sea-froth formed,
My circles fittingly adorned.

Rain-clad I stand and watch the waves.
White horses roll on by and crash
Against the shore, my circles dashed;
Sand heals the wounds I made.

No odds to me, I step within
Another circle, skin alights against my own.
Strong arms, warm and quick to catch,
To hold me here where I belong.

Kezia Thomas, Birmingham, West Midlands

LAUNDRYMA

You had,
Sharp creases
In your jeans
And white socks, for

You took
Your washing
Back for mum
To do, and

Relied
On her, too
For all your
Shopping, but

It's not
So strange
When you know,
It's the result of

Many
Loads of white
Washed tumbled
Household lies, and genes.

Elizabeth Rawson, Solihull, West Midlands

THE OLD MAN

As summer takes its ultimate bow
The old man shivers and bends somehow
To brace himself for winter's chill
Of rain and sleet and snow until
The frozen earth does finally thaw
And he holds his head erect once more
To drink the warmth of promised sun
When winter's chill is finally done
But he must patiently wait for spring
When squirrels wake and blackbirds sing
And only then will the oak tree bud
The old man stands proud, where he's always stood.

Sally Jobson, Brownhills, West Midlands

Sally Jobson said: "My passion for the use and abuse of the English language, nostalgia and a fanatical obsession with pens, inspire all of my work. I love writing whimsical, nostalgic poetry and have had numerous poems published. In addition, I have recently completed my second family saga novel - as yet unpublished. My husband, Phil, daughter, Alex and deranged labrador Phoebe are now immune to my selective hearing and constant scribbling, simply hoping they are not the subject of my latest project. I also write personalised verse for gifts or framing - Details available on 07974 696082."

REFLECTIONS

Look in the mirror, what do you see?
A face, a person, this is me.
I look like this, it's how I appear
But the face isn't me, it's not even near.
What of my thoughts, my life, my mind
An image in a mirror is like one who is blind.

Linda Flowers, Coventry, West Midlands

SPRINGTIME

Of all the seasons I have seen,
Springtime the best has been

Birds back from migration,
Animals out of hibernation.

And in the trees buds begin to bloom,
Showing me I must clean up my room.

Windows are open all around,
Letting in the springtime sound.

Sweeping brushes, digging spades
Singing birds, such busy days

In the fields new lambs are prancing,
New calves and colts a-dancing.

All is freshness all is new,
Yes I love springtime, don't you?

Alan Kavanagh, Kings Norton, West Midlands

JANUARY

January is so very cold
And soft white frost covers the snowdrops
Now gone past as in years of old
Under the soil small beasts lie
And in the snow children tread, so softly
Remember our lives may anytime end
Yet the world goes on in a continuous circle.

Kevin Tonry, Birmingham, West Midlands

ORIGINS

I adore all poetry
A passion that goes back in time
Descending the years to my childhood
Over those hills of mine
Rhyme or not to rhyme
Ever heard that before?
Perhaps 'twas William Shakespeare
Or some other bard from old yore
Each of us should try it
To compose a diminutive rhyme
Really strive to endeavour
You'll see the results in time
Although I'm no eminent poet
Never give up, I cry
Detach myself from criticism
Verbally defy
Ever ponder from where it began
Right here on parchment with quill
Shakespeare, Byron, Rosetti, et al.
Ever onward with cast iron will.

Jacqueline Burke, Darlaston, West Midlands

THE CITY

The streets abound with folks galore
Shopping, rushing; cars race around
Buses too and much, much more
Serve to create that special sound
A city's live, pulsating roar.

Scurrying crowds, all in haste
In every direction
Not a moment to waste
Offices, shops, statues and squares
All serve to attract visitors' stares.

Pigeons fly over, creating a stir
Creating diversion, also a mess
All part of a pattern; with wings awhirr
Providing more interest
Increasing the stress.

And all about, cloud overall
Fumes, pollution, dirt and dust
A traffic-created, funeral pall
Society's creation: but we must
Find a solution - or forfeit all.

F Cutler, Dudley, West Midlands

Dedicated to my dear wife, Pamela, whose interest and enthusiasm helped give me confidence to further my poetical aspirations.

A SORRY SIGHT

We inherited this living earth
but we were not satisfied.
It was not enough
that we should live
not enough
that we could thrive.
We wanted more
and more and more.
We cared not
for any other
And now we stand
a sorry sight
for we have almost
killed our mother.

Jane Swain, Coventry, West Midlands

TO A YOUNG FRIEND ON HER TWENTY-FIRST BIRTHDAY

And so you've reached another milestone on Life's way,
Treading its path of years with grace you've gone;
And no doubt proudly shines your heart today,
As you look back on twice ten years and one.

Oh yes, the time is here at last proud heart in truth,
and surely no dark cloud to dim your radiant smile will
come
Today - for you can wave, that's in your grasp the wand of
youth,
and you may dwell awhile in fair Elysium.

But you must then turn round and with the key,
Unlock the portals leading up to future skies;
And may with you go courage, joy, sincerity,
With which to temper all the sorrow, pain and lies.

Godfrey Nall, Solihull, West Midlands

CHRISTMAS FOR A FIFTIES CHILD

Waking up before it's light
To see the shapes, oh what a sight
Closing my eyes till at light of dawn
I could finally wake on Christmas morn.

There was a sack, full to the brim,
A Rupert annual, how I loved him.
Another doll for my foreign collection,
A talking doll would be perfection.

Opening each present was slowly done,
With a little urging from my mom,
To savour each one enhanced the pleasure,
Of opening the parcels to see the treasure.

To see the knobbly stocking there,
What was inside, I did not care.
The lumps and bumps were so appealing
I scarce could keep myself from feeling.

To reach inside, what an adventure,
From top to toe and in the centre.
And at the bottom would always sit,
An orange, some nuts and a shiny threepenny bit.

Madeleine Williams, Halesowen, West Midlands

THE ELEVENTH DAY

Cries of pain join cries of shame
Searching for answers to heal the pain
Looking to leaders who hurt just the same
We watch in awe through the dust and the rain

See the oceans of children's' tears
So many lives lost, so many years
See the man who risks his life with fear
As sunlight dawns the dust-clouds clear

A father dies whilst a nation cries
People ask how can it fall from the skies?
But though it's crazy I know that it's wise
From the ashes we will watch love rise.

I know you feel the way I do tonight
I know you need the ones you love tonight
I'm sure that love will find a way
To reach out and heal the pain.

Paul Harris, Solihull, West Midlands

Born in Birmingham **Paul Harris** enjoys writing, music and reading. "I began writing songs and poetry when I was around 15 and I have continued ever since," he pointed out. "More recently I have written my first short story. I am heavily influenced by writers and novelists including Paulo Coelho and James Redfield. All my poetry and writing is based around hope and the wish that good will always conquer. I would like to be remembered as somebody who gave more to others than he took in return and who was able to get others to improve their own lives through his words and actions." Aged 37, Paul is a UK sales manager with an ambition to become a successful author of self help and development books for adults and children. He is married to Samantha and they have three children, Amy, Jessica and James.

YOU AND I

I have watched hearts breaking
I have watched love in the making
I have watched people cry
I have watched people die
I have met people who are hard
I have met people who are scarred
I have seen things you wouldn't want to see
I have been places you wouldn't want to be
But overall I have felt something you can't feel.

Heather McCurry, Solihull, West Midlands

THE ADVENTURERS

We came as strangers
Not knowing, just wondering
Hopes high, spirits bright
Trying to anticipate the journeys to come
Breaking down barriers along the way
Thoughts turning towards the moment
Past events, a little further from our minds
Seizing what was present, as an opportunity
Not shrinking at the enormity of the tasks lying ahead

And time softened the edges
Strangers - no more
A place now home
The tasks no longer mountains to climb
But hills and winding valleys
Dreams became realities
Events - the norm

Yet still we wish to venture on
In search of what is yet to come.

Katherine Parker, Wolverhampton, West Midlands

WINTER DUSK

Winter dust falls silently,
An eerie half-light descends.
We know that day is ending
We feel the night approaching.
The sky is painted crimson by the setting sun.
On the horizon the church steeple is painted black.
The bare branches of the winter trees stretch
upwards like a giant's fingers reaching for the sky.
Finally day relinquishes its hold on the light
And the sky turns everything grey,
A grey seagull flies disconsolately homewards,
And grey houses line the road,
So I flick on my headlights
to dispel the oppressive gloom.
The short rule of dusk is over
And kingly night takes his throne.

Anne Harding, Wolverhampton, West Midlands

OUT AT SEA

When you are out at sea
There are most sure to be,
Dolphins dolphins, everywhere,
Dolphins here, dolphins there

"Come and join us", they seem to call,
You reach towards them but you fall,
"We will save you", they start to cry,
They rush towards you, they seem to fly,

You get hold of one, they glide to shore,
They push you onto the sandy floor,
They stay with you till help arrives,
Then slide away into the morning skies.

Samantha Ives, Walsall, West Midlands

REMORSE

They come again and again,
The ghosts of remorse,
That penetrate the heart,
With thorn-like recourse!,
Deep! deep! deep! as sure
as time, and time never sleeps.

But! it needn't be that way
We could "shine" another day
If we blow our weather-vanes for better!

Dorothy Hunt, Solihull, West Midlands

THE LACE DESIGNER

Crystal droppers perfectly formed,
Glinting in the early morning light,
Where dew placed by nature,
Adheres to the finest gossamer,
Spun to perfection,
Its intricate pattern delicate yet strong,

The designer spins with accuracy,
Traversing the masterpiece,
Interlacing the silk threads,
Perfecting knots at precise intervals,
On completion the masterpiece wafts to and fro,
In the gentle breeze,

The architect of this residence,
Now takes up its central position,
Legs finely tuned to any vibrations on the web,
The unsuspecting prey lands upon this lace doily,
Thus captured and imprisoned,
The designer awaits the feast.

Ann Wallace, Wolverhampton, West Midlands

BIRCHILL'S CANAL MUSEUM

So, what can this boatman's mission be,
garrisoned here since nineteen hundred and three
aside Walsall's top lock?
Well, such a hidden gem is Birchill's canal museum.

Here alongside the "cut" can be found this tribute
to navvies and boatmen, borne out of a friendly society.
With only two in the country, 'tis rare indeed.

A full-size narrowboat cabin is contained therein,
alongside decorative artworks, metal and tin.
All examples of lost crafts from Brindley and Telford's age
when goods were transported smoothly and cheaply.

No longer these waterways are used in such ways,
no traffic jams for them, hold-ups, delays.
Powered by the mighty horse pulled by rope,
visible scars cut deep into the fabric of bridges.

During these holidays, when days seem long,
why not go yourself and see
how goods were shipped inland.
It's local and best of all - free.

Mark Dabbs, Walsall, West Midlands

AMAZING ANIMALS

The snake's sizzling snap,
To the cheetah's cheating clap,
To the crocodile's chalky crack,
The lion's long-lasting laugh.

To the elephant's endless electric trunk,
To Tarzan's tough teasing talk,
The parrot's poking purple beak,
To the zebra's zig-zagging zapping stripes.

To the spider's spinning silky web,
To the frog's fidgety freaky fingers.
The baboon's bumpy blazing bottom,
To the cat's creaky crumbling claws.

The dog's dirty dazzling coat,
To the lizard's light lanky lounge,
The grasshopper's glowing glittering antennas,
To the butterfly's beautiful bright wings.

The hyena's hungry hasty howl,
To the monkey's mischievous master march.
The world wouldn't win without wonderful
wildlife.

Aradhna Jaswal, Bilston, West Midlands

TO MY FIRST LOVE

Listen to me now,
I'll tell you how I feel.
I only have one heart to give,
And that is why I'm here.

No wait and listen carefully,
To what I have to say.
I've loved you all these years,
And soon you'll go away.

I just want to say I love you,
No one else but you.
I want us to be together,
From this day and forever.

Hena Begum, Walsall, West Midlands

Born in Lambeth **Hena Begum** enjoys all sports, socialising, music and poetry. "I started writing poetry when I was about 13," she pointed out. "I wrote my first poem as a school assignment and have loved poetry ever since. My work is inspired by my feelings and people around me and my style is biographical. I would like to be remembered as an open-minded, humorous, thoughtful person." Aged 20, Hena is a paralegal with ambitions to spend her career in law, help others and enjoy life. "The person I would most like to be for a day is the comedienne Dawn French because she is so carefree and I would love to meet another comedienne, Ellen Degeneres, as I admire her sense of humour and openness."

A ROSE

A rose
Shall I see the rose as a love affair,
Hidden within the weeds that surround it?
Watch it as it blossoms and grows wild among,
The weeds the only part of life that has colour.
Let the heart stay enclosed in the centre,
Hidden from view by the petals.
The petals being the source of this love.
Each one a romantic word whispered to the night.
Another a look which stirs the mind,
Maybe the other being a movement of seduction.
Who knows where it might end,
All I know is it must be watered with tears,
Nourished by passion,
And sunned with personality.

Louise Nutting, Wolverhampton, West Midlands

TO HAVE AND NOT TO HOLD

To have and not to hold
So hot, yet so cold
To love, but not to keep
To laugh, not to weep
Like a moth to a flame
Only I am to blame
What can I do?
I go straight to you
I've been told you're to have not to hold
To look but not to see
To kiss but never be
The object of your desire
I'm walking on a wire
And there's no one at all to break my fall

Marian Latham, Brierley Hill, West Midlands

WITCHING HOUR

Where does my love go in the witching hour?
The bells chime twelve as the callous fluorescent light flick-
ers on.
We look for the anorexic GQ girl with the studio-lit eyes,
I look for the girl with eyes of night, reflecting only the
moonshine.
Never reflecting our state, never reflecting me.
The beast is always hungry for more,
Beggar always on the doorstep wanting a few more coppers
from your soul.
I hold the information that keeps you from knowing me.

Steven Goodall, Willenhall, West Midlands

THINKING

When we are young
We do not think
Of what the future holds
Old age seems so far away
We have not the time
To stand and stay

As life goes on
The mind does dwell
On how life ends
Will we do well?

There must be something
So why fear death
When everlasting life begins?

Joan Morris, Solihull, West Midlands

WOOKIE

I know that he loves me,
I've noted the signs,
I'm told one should seek,
And body language defines.

He hangs on my word,
Is ever attentive,
And to amuse me,
Is always inventive.

I truly believe
That he's loyal and true,
He interacts with friends,
Be they old, or quite new.

I play hard to get,
And that's to no avail,
He loves me, he shows me,
By wagging his tail.

Alexandra Gail Millington, Aldridge, Walsall, West Midlands

THE TREE

The tree is magical and wise
It is personified by nature
It is old like Methuselah
Yet young in the recourse of time
Its beauty is everlasting,
Picturesque scenery
A carved mantle
A polished table.
Its youthful splendour at Christmas comes forth
We adorn it with winter buds of baubles,
The tree is in flower, summer in summer
And now summer in winter.
The tree is the druid
Simplicity in its life-giving ways.

Steven G Powell, Wolverhampton, West Midlands

Born in Wolverhampton **Steven Powell** enjoys painting, drawing, athletics, writing, cave and mine exploration and hill walking. "I started writing 12 years ago, inspired by the magical sights I have seen during my travels," he explained. "My style is flowing and readable. My influences include Tolkien, Dickens and S Baring Gould. I would like to be remembered as a serious artist and writer." Aged 43, Steven is a carpenter with an ambition to travel through the Grand Canyon so that he can gain inspiration from nature in its raw element. He is married to Katherine and they have one son, Lee. "I have produced two published works on caves and subterranea and have also written a number of poems," Steven added.

TO OLD AGE

Why do we have to age?
Look around, it's all the rage.

Greying hairs,
Comfy armchairs.
Blue rinse tints and butterscotch mints.

It's just another page in life's chapter.
So look forward to it with laughter.

Wendy Glear, Dudley, West Midlands

TIME TO GO

I can see you,
Standing tall,
Broad shoulders,
Proud.

Lying on that hospital bed.
Sunken eyes,
Yellow skin.
All I can do is wait.

Wish I could tell you,
How I really feel,
What you mean to me.

I need to be strong,
Not for you, but for me,
I need you to end it,
Need you to go.

Sabiha Ullah, Birmingham, West Midlands

ER, UM

I remember her saying, sadly,
"I haven't got the words."
So very small and so very serious.
With an ache and with awe
I knew it was true.
I said: "You will, you will."
But I knew I had missed something special.

Now she writes poetry;
Poetry that she and I enjoy.

I know that feeling;
The "not having the words";
The feeling being quicker than the thought
And the thought being bigger than the word.

M A Evans, Castle Bromwich, West Midlands

Dedicated to Chloe J. Time, effort, love and words rush by.
Words and love can last. Here's proof! Choose wisely, use
well.

THE LITTLE BROWN CAR

The little brown car in the toyshop,
In its box it did look so pristine,
Stacked on the shelf with the others,
They all looked so new and so clean.
The little brown car remained on the shelf,
As the others were gradually sold,
The only one left and gathering dust,
It sadly began to look old.
Weeks passed by that rolled into months,
The car then was labelled half price,
The shopkeeper tired of dusting it,
This was his last throw of the dice.
Several weeks later a man came in,
And noticed the little brown car,
He couldn't believe how cheap it was,
For this he had searched near and far.
He knew that this car was extremely rare,
Just one of ten that were made,
The little brown car once unwanted,
In pride of place now displayed.

Andrew Blakemore, Walsall, West Midlands

NANNIE BISCUIT

Great-nan, nan, mum, sister and friend
Always there to lend a helping hand.
At the age of ninety still going.
The golden blood in her veins still flowing.
And this her ninetieth birthday, it shall be.
She's the kindest nan to you and me.
The centrepiece, the jewel of our family crown.
A figurehead and a role model renowned.
A full ninety years of life.
Through happiness and enjoyment
Thirty-seven of them spent as a loyal devoted wife.
Grandad really was the love of her life.
Blessed with five sons, brimming with pride with them
right at her side,
Let us not forget their lovely wives.
Thirteen grandchildren arrived one by one, the first Julie in
1961.
The great-grandchildren too numerous to count.
Even as we speak there's one on the way, it could arrive
any day.
Ever since I could talk, I've always called my nan, Nannie
Biscuit.
She will forever be a special nan to me.

Thomas White, Walsall, West Midlands

Dedicated to a very special Nan, Nannie Biscuit. In celebration of her 90th birthday.

SPRING IS HERE

Singing in the sunshine,
Singing in the rain,
Skylarks flying up above,
Blackbirds trilling songs
of love,
Coming close with heads one side,
To see if we are there,
Little creatures coming out,
To see the magic sun come out,
To see if spring is there,
Tranquillity prevails again,
'Cause spring is in the air.

Florence Thomas, Walsall, West Midlands

HARMLESS GOSSIP

I stay away out of fear
ideas and views will be twisted,
turned, and stabbed into my back.

I find you hidden among true concern
I stay away, prefer to be alone.
Nothing's fair about fair-weather friends.

Rumours spread thick like treacle
suffocating, flocks of arguments fly
flinging sharp words, cutting, killing.

Lives so shallow, gossip rules
Laugh over beer. Think?
Lies and mockery destroy.

Claudine Weeks, Coseley, West Midlands

THE LAST STEAM GIANT

Designed into being in 1938
Class A4 Mallard, number 4468
from Gresley's pen, once sped apace
this awesome loco of style and grace.

100 tons of unbelievable might
schoolboys marvelling - a crackerjack sight
world speed record, proven power
to hold for all time - 126 miles per hour.

In liveried coat of famous blue
grand giant of steam arrives on cue
at each new station for all to see
proud driver and fireman on footplate free.

Streamliners all, planned for speed
Coronation Scot and Mallard lead
from London to Tyneside flying high
1930s their day, now inert they lie.

In York sits Mallard in silent grace
job now done, once more to face
eager schoolboys like fathers before
dreaming of heydays, rushing steam once more!

Clive Bowen, Solihull, West Midlands

BLACKBIRD

A blackbird sang for me today
He perched on high, his feathers sleek.
The sweet voice filling the air,
I stood enraptured.

He sang for me again and again
His voice sweeter still.
I ceased my work and listened hard
Then he flew towards the hill and settled there,
His singing stopped but for a moment then
He flew back and sang to me again.

Elizabeth White, Coventry, West Midlands

NO NEED FOR WORDS

An affluent ambience
Of mutual silence
Between us two
Just me and you
No puss-filled words
Or oozing curds
Of conversation
Bursting sterilisation
Just cosy sentience
Ripe with eloquence
As we sit in place
Face to face
In our MDF castle
Free of hassle
For our bodies shriek
And our eyes speak
All our talk

Gail Sturgess, Birmingham, West Midlands

FAMILY INCREASE

A family increase we have had
Yes, you're right, another lad
He is a real bundle of joy
This seven pounds fifteen ounce baby boy.

He's a little brother for Adam who's five
And couldn't wait for him to arrive
It has been such a long time
Can I take him out to climb?

You'll have to wait till he grows up
First, he must learn his milk to sup
You can hold him, if you're good
But you'll have to wait to play in the mud.

Hold him gently, don't be rough
He's very delicate, not like you, tough
Why mummy, will he break?
No, but to hurt him is a mistake.

What do you think of your little brother
I love him to bits, thank you mother
I know his name is Samuel mummy
But if it's all right with you I'll call him Sammy.

Francis Harrison, Coventry, West Midlands

GROWN UP

No love-worn teddies under foot,
No playing shop and dressing up,
No paddling pool or daisy chain,
No insy, winsy spider game.
No drawings for my kitchen wall,
No conker fights or playing ball,
No blow the candles, make a wish,
No bedtime tale or goodnight kiss.
No tears to wipe, no hand to hold,
No tiny gloves for when it's cold,
No sleepy soul upon my knee,
No little arms that cuddle me.
It never caught this mother's eye,
How fast the years were going by,
Time must have played a trick on me,
You're grown and gone, how can that be?

Gillian Oakley, Kingswinford, West Midlands

EURO ENTERTAINING

The pasta's got loads of garlic,
The vinegar is balsamic,
The tomatoes have to be plum,
The dessert may be laced with rum.

The pizza's boasting a stuffed crust,
Drizzling olive oil is a must,
Melting cheese is mozzarella,
The tiramusu is bella!

The chardonnay's perfectly chilled,
The coffee beans are freshly milled,
The green salad is lightly tossed,
The entertaining art not lost.

Angela Kirby, Coventry, West Midlands

TIME

If I could only stop the hands of time.
Just for a moment, there would be, no more
Hate, no more violence, no more crime. I would
Just have peace among all men, no matter
What colour, creed, race or religion
If I could only stop the hands of time.

Betty Wright, Walsall, West Midlands

LOVE IS

Love is a dream that not only eyes can see
But love is between you and me
Love is what true hearts desire,
And your heart is on fire.
Love is a chemical reaction for people to give one another,
We even experience love between a sister and a brother
Love is a thing that never comes to an end.
Even between you and me my friend.
If you are younger if you are old.
Love is a thing that will never go cold.
Love is a warm feeling inside,
And no one can hide
Love is a game of give and take,
Love is a sexual feeling that we make.
Love is a thing of pure bliss,
We even experience love when we kiss.
Love makes our hearts skip a beat
Love is hot like the summer's heat
Love is near and never far,
Love is bright like a shooting star.

Sarah Jones, Brierley Hill, West Midlands

A HOME BEYOND

There is a home beyond
Where some of my friends have gone
Oh, I would like to be there
With my Saviour I will be free
From this world of sin and pain
All tears will be wiped away
No more sorrows and burdens to bear
My Saviour's gentle voice I will hear
With Him I will rest forevermore

Evette Johnston, Dudley, West Midlands

SUMMER

In jumps the summer, we splash in the pool
Ice creams and ice lollies to keep us all cool
put on our lotions and bathe in the sun
going on holiday, we're all having fun.

Down on the beach, a splash in the sea
a walk in the park, sit under a tree
a stroll in the country, a picnic or two
or just being lazy for an hour will do

Strawberries and cream, oh what a delight
jump in the shower last thing at night
open all windows, let in the air
read a good book, lounge about in a chair

The skies are blue, the sun shines bright
the flowers in bloom, what a lovely sight.
make the most of summer while it's here
then out jumps summer until next year.

Jacqueline Sutton, Walsall, West Midlands

TO THOSE WHO LOVED THE SUMMER

The town in summer grows blue in hue
while we sit and sweat like salad in heat;
Tired, but restless, with nothing to do.
Somewhere the tinkling of an ice-cream van floats across
breezeless air,
chiming like seraphim in a cloudless heaven,
while childish cries ring out the distances between us.
See the sun with his mocking eye
laughing, as the soil cooks and the seas boil.
Every tree and plant harbouring dangers of stings
and allergy-fuelled misery
in a barbecue world of long conversations and short tem-
pers,
while we, the Unhappy Few, sit, sigh and complain.
I wish for downpours, to wash our grime away.

Gemma Styles, Walsall, West Midlands

MOMMIES DAY

Today is a day for mommies everywhere,
To rest and sleep and to lie upstairs,
Today's the day when all kids should be good.
And if they're not, they should be put in mud,
And if, at the end of this hopefully happy day,
You're just not pleased, you have no heart, I say.
Many kids love their mom, I know I love mine,
Although I don't show it all of the time,
Sometimes we shout or row and sometimes we argue,
But there is a love between us that is pure and true,
So, for Mother's Day, mommies enjoy yourselves,
And don't worry about washing or ironing the towels!

Luke Mosley, Birmingham, West Midlands

*Dedicated to my mom for giving me help and support. She
always stands by me and I'll always love her.*

SPEAKING ANOTHER LANGUAGE

What's the point?
Why bother?
I'll do it later.
It's cool.
Don't ask me, ask the brain.
The teachers are all complete fools.
Don't put things up in my bedroom.
I know just where everything goes.
No, I don't need a bin.
Yes, the creased look is in,
So I don't need to iron my clothes.

Julie Sheridan, Birmingham, West Midlands

DAD

The face is wrinkled
The hair is thin.
The bones are brittle,
Under aged, worn skin.
The tastebuds fade,
The eyes grow weak
Hard to smile
Hard to speak.
Knowing is a bitter pill,
That life's caught up,
I'm old not ill.
Be not forgotten is all I ask
Think of me, in your daily task
I've tried to give, in every way
Things in life, for which you pray
And when I'm called.
Do not be sad
I was your buddy
And your dad.

Thomas Ilsley, Wolverhampton, West Midlands

THE ELEMENTS

Earth: My roots search deep in earnest ploy,
To bind myself anew.
But myriad cares detract my aims,
And stifle growth and harvest.
Yet still mother earth embraces me.

Water: It laps my feet, and cools my brow,
Slakes my thirst and bathes my wounds.
Where streams run cold.
And seas plunge deep
Surely, there will my stain remove?

Wind: To my soul brings flight,
Soaring above this restive home,
Seeking aloft some remedy,
That to itself makes known,
Returning cleansed, refreshed, restored.

Fire: To sear and search my inner self,
Inquire beyond my bounds.
To flame, to blaze, to fuse, convert,
Returning to a source unnamed,
All scars removed, renewed.

James Slater, Dudley, West Midlands

LETTING GO

You never even asked where I was going
As I walked out the door.
You didn't imagine what would happen
As you watched me leave.

It has been like this forever.
I do as I please,
I go where I want to go,
I am who I want myself to be.

There must be a word for this.
Some call it freedom,
Trust even,
Respect.

But with you it is something else.
Indifference? Apathy?
Fear of rejection?
Or finally realising that I need you no more?

Why have you let me go so soon,
Though I needed and wanted it?
How could you be so calm,
As I walked out the door?

Alexandra Weston, Birmingham, West Midlands

Born in Birmingham **Alexandra Weston** enjoys art, reading, socialising and walking. "I started writing poetry only recently," she remarked. "I found it a helpful way to express my emotions, which are a great influence on my work as well as family and friends. I would describe my style as a clear reflection of feelings and I would be like to remembered as someone who followed God, kept my faith and let my experiences enhance me." Aged 17, Alexandra is a student with an ambition to be happy in her family and her work. She wishes to be an overseas missionary worker. "The person I would most like to meet is God because he is always there for me and forgives me," she added.

CEREBRAL NEUROSIS

Is there a dark cloud,
Building inside my head?
Is there a disturbance,
An approaching storm?
Will the electric
Forks of lightning
And the deafening,
Concussive thunder
Leave me sifting
Through the remnants
Of my scrambled memories?

Alan J Woodhams, Chelmsley Wood, West Midlands

A VIEW FROM THIS HILL

The hum of the traffic, the lights of the night,
Even in the darkness such a beautiful sight.
Does you mind wander to a time, a time of romance,
adventure so fine?
Does your spirit surge up within you,
While being in this peace infatuated with this view?
Do you feel challenged and renewed?
To achieve more to rebuild.
Do you think on the past, happy thoughts flood through?
Special times, special thoughts coming to you.
Are you looking to the future, what do you see?
Does your future look glorious just like the scenery?
Wherever you look is all you see is hope?
However much the inner turmoil even when your spirit is
broke.
So seize this moment to look beyond your eyes.
Look into yourself you've got the strength to be revived.

Garry Thomas, Halesowen, West Midlands

147

LOVE AND MARRIAGE

Try and get a bloke,
To look after you, for the rest of his life -
Wear low cut tops
And show your thighs.

If you've got any brains -
You don't have to tart yourself up -
You can enjoy your life
And fall in love.

John Carr, Wolverhampton, West Midlands

ALONE

The story's out,
Everyone knows.
You're famous before
You can wriggle your toes.
There are pictures of you
In every magazine,
You've really created
Quite a scene.
The adults are fighting
In the court
While you lie there
Knowing nought.
Will they tell you
When you're grown
That once,
You were not alone
Jody?

Saajida Mehrali, Birmingham, West Midlands

THE BEAUTY OF NATURE

What good is life if we are not aware
That the beauty of nature is for all to share
The sight of swallows swirling by
And a sunset fading in a scarlet sky?

The rustle of leaves on elegant trees
And the scent of flowers in a blissful breeze
Yes! These are the things that prove to me
The beauty of nature for all to see.

To see the hedgehog roam his field
To see what *nature* has to yield
To watch the crafty fox at play
Which thrills my heart throughout the day
And the adder coiled inside a hole
To watch the antics of the vole.

James Turner, West Bromwich, West Midlands

Born in West Bromwich **James Turner** enjoys writing poetry, painting and writing magazine articles. "I started writing poetry mainly after I retired from the teaching profession, to keep my mind active," he explained. "My work is influenced by world events and my love of nature and I would describe my style as ornate and orthodox with rhyme and rhythm. I would like to be remembered as a good artist, good poet and a lover of nature and God." Aged 86, James is married to Heather and they have a daughter, Deborah. "I have written articles for bird magazines for the last 40 years and I have written over 100 poems, many of which have been published."

HAPPILY EVER AFTER

When I am famous I long to be,
In a house on the Cornish coast,
I will sit and gaze at the magical sea,
That's what I will love the most.

I would take my inspiration,
From hearty lasting looks,
At tumbling tides, and stormy skies,
And write about them in books.

My family would live the healthy life,
And feed off the love of the land,
My books would sell, so my heart would swell,
Like the sea rolling onto the sand.

But for now, I'll sit on the balcony,
Gazing out at the motorway,
But that Cornish house with the lovely views,
That's where I'll be some day.

Louise Green, Solihull, West Midlands

One step closer! For Nigel, Megan, Ellie and all the family, with my love.

CASTLES IN THE SAND

In the doorway I stand again,
Watching helpless and alone,
As the castles in the sand wash away,
Caught in the early morning tide.

A lone figure crawls to my feet,
"There is nothing else to do," they say,
But their words ring empty and shallow,
A single voice in an uproar of lies.

Catch the dreams in your hands,
But watch their sands as they drain away,
Sing the notes of a joyful song,
And watch them caught on the breeze.

It is a lifetime of possibilities,
But it takes only a moment of pure regret,
To take the hopes and wring them in the river,
The colours draining and fading in the currents.

Set up your scaffold,
Build the walls of time high,
Then watch all your hard work crumble,
Like castles in the sand.

Ian Griffiths, Wolverhampton, West Midlands

SEASONS

When autumn leaves begin to fall
And twilight shadows deepen.
Our thoughts turn to a cosy fire
With glowing coals and flames a-leapin'.
For soon those icy winds will blow
Bringing the first of winter's snow
Which then as though with magic wand
Transforms the earth to fairy land.
While silently beneath the snow
Nature works her miracle
The snowdrops peep the heads and then,
Suddenly its spring again.

Joan Garbett, Walsall, West Midlands

I THOUGHT

I thought that I was over you,
but then I saw your face.
I've realised my love for you,
is still there.
You're always at the back of my mind,
I think about you all the time.
I thought that I was over you,
but then you rang my phone,
your voice echoed in my ears.
I thought that I was over you,
when I saw you in the street.
I guess my love will always stay,
as much as I detest.
I couldn't get rid of your voice,
or face out of my head.
Sometimes I wish I was dead.

Gemma Martin, Bilston, West Midlands

I'M A LITTLE ROBOT

Programmed, programmed, I'm at school
Doing what I'm told and following the rule
Sit down, stand up do as I say
Come back again to spend another day

Programmed, programmed, I'm at work
Pick up, put up you don't shirk
You'll do as I say, I'm the boss around here
Do as you are told do I make myself clear!

Programmed, programmed, the politicians' way
You must pay this, you must pay that, and you mustn't
disobey
Sit down while you watch your favourite football team
Just sit and clap, we want no scream!

Don't park your car, we'll clamp and fine
Because your life, it's mine, mine, mine
We'll watch you from birth and give you a number
Any trouble and you'll be in lumber

We're watching and watching, big brother's after you
All of our life we're living in a zoo
Control me, control me, you don't care
I'm a little robot, ready for warfare.

Peter Hill, West Bromwich, West Midlands

THE PARACHUTIST

Down, down, faraway down
Like puppets on strings or birds
without wings,
Dots on the landscape of far
distant trees,
Billowing canopies enveloping wind,
Like yachts in full sail on cumulus
seas,
Swinging and swaying in gentle decent,
The parachute jumpers in gala event.

Beryl Powles, Birmingham, West Midlands

LOVE IS

Love is knowing what a person will say,
Before they even open their mouth.

Love is a relationship that grows stronger,
With every argument shared.

Love is accepting all their annoying little habits,
And loving them all the same.

Love is fireworks and sea-horses,
Roses and confetti,
Drizzling rain and warm sunshine.

Love is a word of contrasts,
And the most natural human emotion in the world.

Love is what has kept us together for all these years,
And what will keep us together for all those to come.

Melanie Dillon, Birmingham, West Midlands

NAN

The gates are open to heaven above,
She has risen to the land of love,
No one cry, it's all okay,
She has passed on Judgement Day.

Her faith in God, she was brave and bold,
She's worth more than frankincense, myrrh and gold.
She may not be on earth, but she'll always be in me,
If life were a lock she would be the key.

Matthew Jackson, Wolverhampton, West Midlands

*Dedicated to Nan, whom I loved and respected and my
English teacher, Miss Baker at Uplands School, for her
inspiring influence.*

VENOMUSS

Predator stalks, close behind
Watch it sliver, watch it wind.

Prey is trapped, about to die
Stalker smiles, rears up high.

In a flash, the neck goes crack
Predator swift, fast attack.

Venom courses through the veins
Consciousness, the prey then feigns.

Muscles twitch then start to cramp
Victim spasms in the damp.

Not much life, dark and dain
The prey writhes about in pain.

Matthew Shilvock, Stourbridge, West Midlands

I PRAY

I pray for peace and understanding
In this world of hate and war.

I pray for everlasting love
Stretched between the rich and poor.

I pray for forgiveness and equality
And courage when faced with fear.

I pray that I may see God's face
When I feel the end is near.

Catherine Kerr, Darlaston, West Midlands

HUNGER

There's bread on the table
There's never any jam,
Plenty of beef dripping,
Never any ham
Tea leaves in a caddy
Weak tea brewing in a metal pot.
Made with boiling water
It never stays very hot,
Milk in a little jug
It's started to go sour
A grandfather clock in the corner
Just about to strike the half hour
You know it's nearly time for tea
There's silence as you sit at table
Only broken by the sound of the clock
As it strikes half past three
Oh grandma don't you know
I'd rather have jam and bread for tea.

M Nickson, Coventry, West Midlands

PASSING BELLS

The night grows dark,
Smoke from the chimneys rises into the night.
You can feel it in your heart.
The tolling of the passing bells.

Restless warriors walk in the night,
Dreaming of families long gone. .
Now cold.
Seeing what they fought for, vanished in the night.
The green grass turned red.
A golden glow from the sunset
A promise of the dawn.
The memory is fresh but life carries on.

Why the world is cold I don't know.
In our hearts we live in the past.
We call for golden days and the wars they fought.
We call for better times to come again,
A circle never ending.
The bells always chiming.
Endless?

Peter Hawkins, Solihull, West Midlands

HER

To express and define the essence of her
I can poorly convey with mere words.

If my heart had a voice
It would sing heaven's joy
Every time she steps into my world.

Never before has a lady so sweet
Inspired my heart to go sing.

Of love's magic so wild,
Holy joy, heaven's scent.
Oh I dream that tomorrow may bring.
Her to me.

Stephen C Page, Darlaston, West Midlands

Stephen Page said: "I am a singer/songwriter and self pro-
claimed gipsy. I find my inspiration from a variety of life
experiences but mainly my spiritual journey, belief in
Christ, travel and romance. This is my first published poem
and was inspired by a beautiful dancer, her grace, sensual-
ity and spirit I felt were 'the perfect essence of femininity'.
It is usually when my soul is free from the mundane mech-
anisms of society that the words flow. Travels brings with it
a fantastic sense of freedom, a true sense of liberation and
a way to get in touch with our true selves."

TO A DEAR DEPARTED FRIEND

How could fate decree such an end?
For a man so nice our heart-strings rend
Your sudden departure leaves a huge gap
As your wife and three cats search in vain for your lap
Oh gentle giant, oh prince amongst men
Our fondest wish is we will meet again

Geoffrey Hughes, Aldridge, West Midlands

WE'RE FOOTBALL CRAZY

He should have had a yellow card,
Where were the ref's eyes looking?
We all agreed and shouted out,
Why was the ref not booking?
The game was played by all to win,
But football was in second place,
'Cos some used hands to pull and push,
I don't know how they could show their face;
A penalty was not to be,
The captain looked bemused,
He hit the ground in disbelief,
We all the ref accused;
Let's hope the rules are reinforced
And refs and players go through the mill,
They should be kept upon their toes,
'Cos we like to watch a game of skill;
Jut remember lads to play your best,
That's all that you can do,
And if the ref should disagree,
We don't mind tackling him too!

Mary McPhee, Stourbridge, West Midlands

REMEMBER ME

Remember me
The one who loves you from afar,
The one who lies awake
Night after night,
Wishing upon a star.

Remember me
But, not only as an afterthought,
But as being the one!
Remember, you have my heart,
When all is said and done.

Remember me
Oh! Keeper of my heart,
My soul, my inspiration
You truly are my guiding light,
When I feel in isolation.

Remember me
I'm the one, with depth of feeling.
Remember me
When life gets too tough,
When you're searching for a meaning, remember me.

Anne-Marie McDonald, Birmingham, West Midlands

FOR MY LOVE

Tell me what you want from me
My dearest, dearest friend.
I would give you your heart's desire
Broken dreams I'd try to mend.

Give me your hand when you walk alone
My dearest, dearest friend
I will never let you down
I will love you to the end.

I'll never let you be afraid
My dearest, dearest friend
I'll always hold you close to me
As along life's path we wend.

A lifetime we have been together
My dearest, dearest friend
And all I ever ask of you
Is you'll love me to life's end.

Mary Bagley, Halesowen, West Midlands

DREAM WORLD

It is a dream world coming to life,
A dream world, where the stream
Falls into the pool in slow motion.
Bubbles slip down like a string of crystal beads
Filling my head with remembering and emotion.
The late days of winter soon becoming spring
Stirs my desire to be with you,
And love you as I always will
Love you beneath the trees
Watching changing patterns when my eyes are open,
But when my eyes are closed, feeling only
My great eternal devotion.

Betty Harper, Shirley, Solihull, West Midlands

ASK

I'm here says a voice in the silence
I am waiting for you to call
I am here to ease your pathway
I am here to cushion your fall
I am here to dry those sobbing tears
To ease your troubled heart.
If I am here for you my dear
We should not be apart

Will you listen to my voice now,
Will you answer when I call?
Will you let me help you on your way,
Whatever my befall?
My purpose is to comfort you,
To help with every task.
And all you really have to do,
Is close your eyes and ask.

Anne Priest, Halesowen, West Midlands

EXISTENCE IN ANTITHESIS

It's obvious that you're in love with her,
Though only through your hate for him.
You exist in antithesis,
Hate and life, love and death,
Never finding a middle ground
To breathe and be free.
And if you didn't love her,
Would you still hate him?
Would you know who you are?
Undefined by extremes of emotion,
Unmoulded by these polarised passions
That aren't really you at all,
But them.

Kirsty Saunders, Coventry, West Midlands

LIFE

Life is for living,
Life is for giving,
For caring and sharing,
With no misgivings.

Life passes by so quickly,
So try to live it richly,
It's your day, so have your say,
Even though it may be quickly.

Life doesn't last forever,
Life's about saying maybe or never,
So while we're here,
We'll raise a cheer:
Salute life while we are still here.

Clare Coleman, Walsall, West Midlands

UNTITLED

Haemorrhaging sky
blood-blossoming birds of light
escape the sunset.

Mark Sanderson, Walsall, West Midlands

CHRISTMAS THOUGHT

Missing you more each day time neither heals nor mends
My sorrow and thoughts turn to you
Who could envisage a day without you? So quickly time
passes
Yet you are still with me. Today is Christmas Day and all I
am
And all I ever will be is with me now surrounded by my
family
It is only now I understand you, how proud we are you and
I
We share our thoughts when I look at my son I see the
same as
You saw in me. I look at my love and I feel the same as you
did
For my father. If age gives us this grace then I am fortunate
I thank you for my life I thank you for my memories I
thank you
For who I am and I thank you for being with me on
Christmas Day.
Happy Christmas mom and dad

Stephen Holdnall, Brierley Hill, West Midlands

FIRST STEPS

Mother's arms reach out, in case
he should fall.
His first steps, one, two, three, four.

Remembering and smiling when he began
to talk.
Another cherished moment is fulfilled.
Now he's begun to walk.

Dorothy Ann Parker, Solihull, West Midlands

INTO OUR HISTORY

It was with a sad and heavy heart,
We watched Your Majesty's funeral start,
A gun-carriage carried you on your way,
To the service in Westminster Abbey this sad day.

Grateful for your one hundred and one years,
But still, we couldn't help our tears,
A mixture of sadness and thanksgiving,
For a life so full of living.

A queen, a mother and a grandmother too,
A life dedicated to service were you,
We saw the courage, dignity and strength,
To help good causes you'd go to "length."

To a standstill in silence the country came,
To pay their respects at your very name,
For the sadness we feel, there is no mystery,
As the castle gates close,
And you're driven into our history.

Wendylyn Broadbent, Wolverhampton, West Midlands

HUMAN ANGEL

My love, you will never know
How much I thank the Lord
For sending you to me.
You were there through it all - my private hell
That no one else saw
Because I could not let them.
Only you did I tell
And you looked in my eyes and told me
You believed in me
That you were not going anywhere
That we would see it through together.
Your faith saved me
Your love gave me a
Reason to live
A reason to hold on,
To fight and to win.
Your belief was my rock
It never wavered - was so strong.
And this I now know to be true -
There are human angels in this world
For I have found one in you.

Mahmuda Yasmin, Birmingham, West Midlands

THE SQUIRREL

The squirrel is a frisky thing,
I often see him in the spring.

He climbs the trees so green and tall,
I sometimes think that he will fall.

I see him not on a summer's day
but then I have my friends to play
the noise they make keeps him away, says mummy.

In the autumn he's as busy as can be,
jumping about from tree to tree, gathering
nuts and food to eat, which he buries in a hole he made
with his feet.
He does this every autumn season and we know he has a
reason.

The winter months are chilly days and out of sight the
squirrel stays.

Jean Spink, Walsall, West Midlands

SANTA

There are loads of presents under the tree
Not all for you not all for me,
It's time to thank Jesus for us all living
And to other people just for giving.
It's the time of year for getting together
And also for getting presents maybe some leather
In front of an open fire with stocking on the wall
While you're waiting for Santa hoping for his call
You must go to sleep and rest your eyes, that's it.
And he will come with Rudolph's nose lit,
In the morning when you're wide awake
Remember not to always take.

Robyn Mosley, Birmingham, West Midlands

SEASONS OF LIFE

The spring of life seems far away
Nothing to do but sing and play
Waiting till those warmer days
Learning all the easiest ways
Then the years of blossom and bloom
No thought of any forthcoming doom
The winds of autumn then arrive
Weathered, beaten, exhausted with drive
Has it really been that long
Since our life was full of song?
Nothing wrong with slowing down
No regret, or need for frown
Before you know the winter's here
Not to say the rest's not dear
Even in the dark of night
Comes that shimmering flash of light.

Malcolm Davies, Dudley, West Midlands

IT WENT BY SO FAST

I wonder if, when I get old will I still wander in museums and
there have stories told
of the artist I never was, of loves I found, and loves I lost
friends who ran in water deep, enemies who plagued my sleep,
I hope my interest can still be peaked
with stroke of brush, with stroke of touch.
I'll sit and drink, the newest drinks
still unsure of what to think,
designs that have overtaken me, fret not artist you'll soon be
free.

I'll watch the youth waste their time, "Wonder what I did with
mine,"
my laughs and shocks, my one night stands
love of a woman, lust of a man
faces in kaleidoscope
no photo or oven-burnt memento
it's all in here, all still clear
I wish I'd cherished you my dear.

Music changes, the beat remains, I have none to whom my
song shall stay
except these words, children true.
I wonder if, when I get new
I'll remember my stories, so I can tell you.

Martin P Burns, Birmingham, West Midlands

Born in Leamington Spa **Martin Burns** is a 25-year-old artist
with an ambition to find his sanctuary. "I started writing poet-
ry when I was very young," he explained. "I realised that my
written words were more interesting than spoken - to me, at
least. I like to turn my everyday experiences into something
mythic. My work is influenced by the way in which I surprise
myself and life surprises me. I would describe myself as a
painter with words, putting my vision into words. My hobbies
include people, music, movies and adventures. My biggest fan-
tasy is to find a peaceful state and my biggest nightmare is to
be forgotten."

THE MAY DAY SHOW

At the village fete on the first of May
The children gave a dance display
Round and round the maypole they twirled
Making patterns with ribbons as each one unfurled

Morris dancers dressed in white
With bells and handkerchieves clutched tight
And comic hats with a coloured feather
Waved hankies high as they danced together

The archers showed skill with arrows and bow
As they aimed at targets placed in a row
Mr Punch with his stick was clowning around
And the children screamed as they sat on the ground

Clog dancers, folk dancers, acrobats too
Entertained one and all as they flocked to view
The fiddler played "The Miller of Dee"
And the children clapped and danced with glee

All of this happened in days of yore
May Day celebrations are sadly no more
Tradition vanished long long ago
But I'll always remember the May Day show

Lorna Evans, Walsall, West Midlands

*Dedicated to my dear friend, Ruby, a lovely lady who is
always ready to help in time of need.*

ICICLE GRASS

Snow solidly on ground
cold day and dry
a line of black bare trees
colourless winter sky
church tower sharply raven-black
We crossed village green a serene
square of cottages and their
roofs snow-moulded and white
lawns shaded with pin strokes
of icicle grass soft
snow creaking at
each footfall

Steve Urbanski, Coventry, West Midlands

ANIMALS

Dogs have brilliant eyesight,
For a female, stags fight.
Cats scratch with their claws,
Horses stand on all fours.
Fish, instead of legs, have fins,
Birds, such as swans, have wings.
Pigs are noisy when they eat,
Ostriches have funny feet.
Rats can cause diseases,
Mice like all kinds of cheeses.
From cows, you can provide milk,
From glow-worms, you can make silk.
Snakes sometimes can be vicious,
Chicken, to eat, is delicious.
Jaguars, how fast they run,
Animals, so many of them.

Rosie Thomas, Walsall, West Midlands

ONE NIGHT STAND

This was our first meeting, oh temperamental friend.
Twenty-three hours with you, I find I have to spend.
Last night in the sunset, we drifted, all was calm.
The wind caressed my skin, the air was fresh and warm.
Seducing with your gentleness, you let us ride upon;
Your back which bore us up with ease, we floated on and
on.
When daylight came and I awoke, a peaceful night had
passed.
But now your temper in full swing, against my window
crashed.
The ship flew up and then sank down, but we still dared to
roam.
To our distant destination, amidst your rabid foam.
We cut through waves which threatened us, we did not
dare to stall.
A "Bronco Billy" holding tight, determined not to fall.
'Tis obvious, oh mighty sea, you do not beg us to stay.
We have spent our night together, you want us on our way.

Nuressa Bessell, Solihull, West Midlands

SAND

A timeless landscape, warm soft sand,
static until disturbed by gentle winds,
forming patterns as of snowdrifts.
Sand, coloured sand until lit by early
morning sun creating golden peaks and
shadowed hollows.
Unruffled sand until broken by movement
of man or beast causing a powdery disturbance
and replacement of grains.
A foot or hand disappears into soft sand
to reappear with granules pouring through
fingers and toes to recreate a different
surface.
Such minute particles, which have taken
millions of years to break down.

Joan Leggett, Birmingham, West Midlands

INSPIRATION

So I'm sitting here, the page is blank.
It's you, this leaflet, I have to thank.
Trying to write from the heart of me,
My most inspiring poem for this anthology.

Must it be not "so long" in verse.
Too many words, this is getting worse.
I haven't already written one I can send,
That fits right in, or that I could even amend.

So here I am, blank page and pen,
Trying to give out my thoughts, and then
Hey, looks like I've nearly done it.
Just hope it's good enough, have I won it?

Mike Cowsill, Birmingham, West Midlands

THE SHADOWS AWAKE

The industrious world tries to hold on,
But the twilight hour strikes and all is gone,
The shattered shadows pattern the sky,
And nothing is heard except a vehicle's cry.

The desolate street is awoken with drunken louts,
Shuddering echoes are heard from their obnoxious shouts,
Broken bottles in a chain make their path,
The street is preparing for a rampage of their wrath.

The shadow disintegrates at the sun break,
The lights rejuvenate and the humans awake,
The sky blanket falls apart,
As the people dress for a fresh start.

The darkness is abolished leeway for the night,
But the stars, the moon and the shadows get ready for
tonight.

Virginia Hancock, Wolverhampton, West Midlands

A LOOPHOLE IN THE DESERT

One tree, it stands, with folded hands,
Twisted, gnarled and weathered
And on one arm, a rope there hangs
A loophole in the desert
And there below, lie sea dog's bones.
Licked clean by sandstorm winds,
The sky above, she gathers up
Her skirts azure in crinoline,
Melting in the lakes of salt,
On amber stones, she walks towards
The next oasis, shimmering.

Emma Louise Cartwright, Sutton Coldfield, West Midlands

HOME

The summer crazed garden sprawled unconfined
Green covered gravel, all quiet as a mouse
In the clashing of colour, pale columbine twined
With ivy reaching the rotting tree-house
Where two hid away until called for tea
Then scrambled to race, all branches astir,
So still in their sorrow when four became three
Life rang the changes that left only mother.

Trebles of children piercing her reverie
Striking a chord of distant delight, yet
In tune with malaise and dusty redundancy
Old faded chintz and misty grey net.
After final appraisal events followed fast
Decidedly all for the best, hers alone
The empty house echoed lament for the past
Heart-sure, there is nowhere better than home.

Sheila Manley, Coventry, West Midlands

JOURNEY UNDER THE WAVES

Diving down deeply to the depths
Bubbles bursting bottle-nosed dolphins breathe
Fishes find food in coral
Whales whip water, wild whales!
Sharks swim like spies searching
Caves cold cavernous dungeons
Wreck with their ornament, windy water
Treasure trunks tricking divers, they're empty.

Oliver Thomas, Walsall, West Midlands

WHAT AM I?

I travel by day and hunt by night
You know I'm there but I'm out of sight
I cannot hurt you but I might
What am I?

I am big for my kind
I have a good mind
I never know what I might find
What am I?

I am quite rare
Live here and there
Could kill a bear
What am I?

I am as black as coal
I have no soul
What am I?
Here's a clue, I have eight legs and live in rainforests.

Joclyn Tolley, Walsall, West Midlands

HEART OF GOLD

My mother has a heart of gold
she shows it with her love,
she brought up eight children
in the good times and the bad;

She wiped away our tears
if frightened by the dark,
and hugged us warmly,
if falling over in the park,

I know at ninety one,
it may seen a large sum,
but it's no age at all
for an ever-loving mum.

Derek Gardner, Coventry, West Midlands

THINGS THAT WILL NEVER HAPPEN

In this blue sky, big and vast
I won't be flying by wing's trust
never will I go to sea
roam and sing as do fishes three
as dew slowly touches the grass
rain - rain gives a jolly brass
I will not be falling on
by my darling's window day and dawn
like the tree with thousand tusks
experience a million dusks
I will not stand still
as thee wise who see but feel
or the life I led past
never, again may I have it cast.

Sreeman Barua, Birmingham, West Midlands

177

IN THE BAG

So still among the wind-stirred leaves,
Eyes that never saw the light of day
Shut tight against the breaking dawn.
Chipolata arms and legs protrude
From a plastic shopping bag.
Squirrels nuzzle tiny finger nails,
Then scamper off to stock their larders.
Cool autumn rain falls gently, washing
Crimson stains of innocence that define
A life on earth which might have found
A cure for cancer, a formula for peace,
Or simply celebrated the joy of spring.

John C Bird, Solihull, West Midlands

BIRTHDAY

Age she calls though unrequested
Her clues were given
In tasks more rested

As well you ought to think thereon
Not saddened by the year that's gone
But on her visit
Like as a gift
The stronger dream on which to drift

Nor brighter could a blue sky be
Without the glow
That age sets free

However then would light I see
Without this day
Time owes to me.

R C Kelly, Solihull, West Midlands

LIFE WITH MEANING

What is the purpose of our life,
If we let worry bring on strife?
Get up with our minds full of stress
And live the day unhappy no less.

The mind the body controls, awake or asleep
If we don't think positively we are sheep.
Think goodness not pessimistic thoughts
And we will eliminate all faults.
Be happy, laugh and sing
Banish negativity's sting.

Help others to overcome their woes,
To conquer all the mental foes.
We alone have the power to live
Be sure we have the means to give.

If only all people in this earth
Lived like this life would be worth
More than possessions and wealth
We all should help others to help ourselves.

R Warrior, Walsall, West Midlands

A SUMMER PLACE

The daffodils are blooming to herald in the spring,
Enticing thoughts of summer days and swallows on the
wing.
The springlike scent is in the air, anticipation rises
For all the summer days to come and all of their surprises.

Oh! how I love the summer and all the days of ember,
And all the wondrous things in store that I shall long
remember.
Trees burst forth and flowers too and all the fields are
crowded;
The scent of jasmin in the air leaves woodland softly
shrouded.

This is a place where I would dwell and never onward ven-
ture,
Summer with its restful days leaves nothing there to cen-
sure.
If I could choose a time to hold in memories sweet encap-
ture,
Then summer's place is where I'd be in green and gold
enrapture.

Beverley Hill, Wednesbury, West Midlands

TWILIGHT

Now is the twilight time, now is the hour
The deep bells toll from village parish tower.
Now is the time of quiet and of peace,
The tranquil time when daylight's rigours cease.

A thousand summers' suns condense to make
This one last hour of sunlight on the lake
By whose meandering path a single soul
Completes a rustic scene - idyllic, whole.

The scent of wood-smoke thick and rich and sweet
In veil-like mist settles upon the street.
Now is the time when clouds, set off by light
Against a deepening sky, draw in the night.

Now is the end of innocence and youth.
What man would not pause here if he knew how
To stop the endless march of time and truth?
Now is the twilight time, and this the hour.

Rachel Evan, Leamington Spa, Warwickshire

CAN YOU TAME A DINOSAUR?

Can you tame a dinosaur? I want one for a pet
I've asked my mum and all she says is I want doesn't get.

A winged Pterodactyl, now that would be so cool
I'd train it single-handedly to fly me into school
Triceratops are cuties, horny prongs upon their head
A baby one would surely fit quite nicely in our shed

I bet a Brachiosaurus would soon lend itself to tricks
I'd slide down its long neck and train it to fetch sticks
But best of all, the dinosaur that everyone respects,
I'd better every bully with Tyrannosaurus Rex.

So, can you tame a dinosaur? I'd like one for a pet
I've asked mum but all she says is I want doesn't get.

Helen Yendall, Coleshill, Warwickshire

THE SACRAMENT

'Twas the glow of the spirit
Gorging in the breast

Calmness, peaceful remedies
Of flow like rivers

Stillness within body and soul

Addressing the outside world
Without blemish

Sublime, perfection, unscathed

Yvonne Bloor, Stoke-on-Trent, Staffordshire

LADY OF THE LAKE

I have seen her dance upon the water;
Beneath the light of a pregnant moon,
Rising like her Excalibur
This Vivienne.

Ivan Latham, Stoke-on-Trent, Staffordshire

PEDESTRIAN

Let's give the cities back to the people
Street and square and tall church steeple.
Some seats where they can take their ease
With shopping baskets on their knees.

Let's give them space where they may wander
Peaceful spots to sit and ponder
Maybe a fountain, or a tree
Let all their zones be traffic-free.

Let's give them parks not planned for cars
Pavement cafes and coffee bars
Familiar places where they can find
A sense of being and peace of mind.

Let's make our cities safe for strolling
With young policemen foot-patrolling;
If civic pride is what we lack
We need our cities, let's give them back.

Winifred Saha, Wolverhampton, Staffordshire

MY BROTHER'S LOVE

My brother died so sudden three years ago,
It cut my heart, it was such a shock,
I felt so angry and hurt why did he have to die,
Leaving his sister too numb to cry?
No time even to say goodbye.
I was so full of pain, so angry it cut like a knife,
I couldn't see me living my life the same again,
He was so full of life, fun to be around,
So close to my kids, who looked up to him like a dad.
The best brother a sister could ever have.
I'll never forget that day God called his name,
Stephen Lowther, my brother not to be seen again,
What keeps me going is my brother's love
Watching over me from heaven above.
So Stephen if you're looking down
Remember you'll always stay with me
In my heart and memories
I'll always love you
Your loving sister.
Alison.

Alison Lowther, Tupsley, Herefordshire

CIRCUS

Tubes
Colourful tubes
Grange Hill, Ealing Broadway, Heathrow
The blue one
Piccadilly
The same man, in the same place. Help
Covent Garden, draw me
Eros
Help with the drinks
Wimbledon, every year
Hendon
Finchley Road
Shopping, Shopping, Shopping
Tottenham Court Road
Bookshops, MacDonalds
People so busy
Life so short
Cafe Rougé
And the lights

Louise Clay, Hereford, Herefordshire

THE SUICIDE BOMBER

Out from the clear blue sky he came
Plunging down to death and shame.
Extermination was his aim
On that fateful day.

Handsome, young and brave was he,
Full of zeal and fancy free.
Little did he know that he'd be
Forgotten in the morning.

He'd been told to take control,
He would give his heart and soul.
New York City was his goal.
Death would be his glory.

Elisabeth Snelling, Whitchurch, Shropshire

UNFORGETTABLE

Riding a homeless unpretentious hesitant homebound
train,
A silvery estuary flings open enchanting welcoming arms
again.
Wavelet reflected diamonds crisply carefree dazzle unex-
pectedly,
Sparks of Sol's providence, granted freely and sincerely
Upon wealth and impoverished together sharing that
moment.
Yet, though granting such a searing and impressive a testa-
ment,
I remain unmoved, haunted still by your significant smile,
Which though of necessity being covert, bespoke no hint of
guile.

R J Neale, Telford, Shropshire

SPREADING

Can you see the ripples, wider and wider,
The water disturbed with a pebble so small,
From stillness to life on and on.
Do we make a difference?
Just a small pebble in a large pond.
If we link each vibration with more pebbles,
In line will we reach the lonely,
The needy the under-developed in time.

Helen Brown, Rugby, Warwickshire

SUN TIME

Laughter mingled with the calls of swifts
Enjoying July and its brightness.
Ground-bound bantams pecked and scratted.
Seemingly oblivious to their noisy cousins.
Their soft, satisfied, chucking, contrasting,
Highlighting a world apart.
Yet both, jungle-wise,
Held the knowledge of
Hungry alien predators.
Only the sky-peppering dots
In the blue English sky
Had seen an equatorial sun.
But the rooster, gaudy, and exotic,
Challenged the world
With his primeval jungle call.
Then our laughter
Seemed to merge
With the birds' cries
We were complete.

Edward Kibbler, Warwick, Warwickshire

DOGS

Dogs are furry, friendly, cute,
They have never-ending tums
And when greeting one of their own kind
They sniff each other's bums.

Now for them it's just a natural act,
Quite normal for the doggy race,
But be careful when they give you love
They always lick your face.

Rikki Nicholls, Kidderminster, Worcestershire

CANINE ELEGANCE

One could not call him, elegant,
However kind one felt;
Any skinnier and he would be
Little more than a belt
The face? well battle-scarred,
Had challenged many a foe,
The shredded ears were evidence
Of times he'd had a go.
Yet something there attracted us
As he lay on his bed,
While the other dogs barked or whined,
He barely raised his head.
We called him and encouraged him
Until he approached the wire door,
He sniffed and licked our fingers,
His eyes saying much more.
We were hooked, without a doubt,
He was the dog for us,
All he needed was some healthy meals
And maybe a little fuss.

David Clarke, Meir, Staffordshire

IN THE GARDEN

It's quiet in the garden,
When the children are at school,
And you're at work,
From dawn till dark;
I hear the song thrush,
And the lark.
I smell the flowers,
Their scent is sweet.
I feel the grass beneath my feet.
I feel so lonely by myself;
Here, at home, alone.
It's quiet in the garden,
But I wish you'd all come home.

Jacqueline Massey, Seabridge, Staffordshire

FLASHOVER

Raging, burning
Whirring
Senses spinning,
Reeling,
They leap screaming
Clawing at the darkness depths,
Searching for endless life.
Life of elements,
Raw, natural elements,
Most basic
Most beautiful evil.
Death following
Panting, begging
They breathe.

Beverley Welsh, Stoke-on-Trent, Staffordshire

PEACE AND QUIET

I am sitting here all alone
So peaceful and quiet
I wander around for things to be done
It's so peaceful and quiet
The TV has so many channels
But I still feel alone
I go for a swim to the pool
Even that
Is so peaceful and quiet
It is nearly time for the peace to end
I am so alone
It is time
To pick the kids up
No more peace and quiet.

Lisa Biddle, Redditch, Worcestershire

FOR MUM WITH LOVE

Mother meant so much to me,
when alive she would always be
there for me by phone or letter
and always make me feel much better.

Now she is gone and I miss her so
but whenever my spirits are really low
I remember my mother through the years
the happy times and sometimes the tears.

But why feel so sad when this I know
that whilst I'm still here on earth below
she is in heaven with Lord Jesus above
and do you know, I still feel her love.

Celia F Brown, Hereford, Herefordshire

MIRAGE

I arose
from troubled sleep
and saw your image
shimmering
in the dissolving
light of day.
My hand
reached for you,
my heart
yearned for your touch.
Outside
the dull and prosaic morning
drifted on,
unsung, uncaring,
quite unaware
of your pure presence.

Paul Portmann, Tenbury Wells, Worcestershire

THAT SMALL SPACE

In that small space
I see you hidden
Your outer shell forgotten
The painted clown is off stage
The little boy is grown
The domain's king has fallen
The doubted son has been found
In that small space
I can see you
Behind all that is shown
Your self is discovered, the man is known
In that small space.

P J Kemp, Hereford, Herefordshire

A CHAUCERIAN ROUNDEL

The flag flew in the city square,
The sky, it had a leaden cast;
As people slowly, quietly massed.

Folks stood, remembering there,
Everyone with eyes downcast;
The flag flew in the city square.

Almost everyone had a memory to share,
Of a princess whose life had passed;
Fluttering in the breeze at half mast
The flag flew in the city square.

Frank Pavitt, Leominster, Herefordshire

SUMMER'S FAREWELL

A red kite ghosts across the rustling moor
A multitude of swallows swarms skyward
No passports, no maps, no money, no food.
Guided to their home by an unseen force.
The moorland heather's glory is fading
And ochre-edged ferns prepare for dormance
Awaiting bluebells' resurrection time.
Damp slowly rises from the mossy bogs
Where frogs explore and linger pensively.
Day disappears, a sense of loss pervades,
And another autumn is harvested.
As the golden orb slowly sinks downwards
The distant horizon fuses with sky,
Soon the lunar searchlight will beam earthwards
In the magical stillness peace will reign.

Wendy Dedicott, St Johns, Worcestershire